Discover Functional JavaScript

An overview of Functional and Object Oriented Programming in JavaScript

Cristian Salcescu

2

Discover Functional JavaScript

Discover Functional JavaScript

An overview of Functional and Object Oriented Programming in JavaScript

Cristian Salcescu

History:

May 2019 First Edition

To my parents, Viorica and Gheorghe

Contents

Chapter 15: Method decorators   141

Chapter 16: Waiting for the new programming paradigm   149

Preface

JavaScript has become one of the most important programming languages. It is important from many points of view:

- It is easy to learn. The beauty of the language stays in its simplicity.
- It is the first language to bring functional programming to the mainstream.
- It offers a new way of doing object oriented programming without classes and prototypes.

JavaScript is popular as being the language of the browser. At the same time it is a powerful and expressive programming language.

This is a book for developers eager to make a foundation of functional programming in JavaScript and whom want to learn a new approach of building encapsulated objects.

Online code examples

Many code examples from this book, but not all, are available at https://github.com/cristi-salcescu/discover-functional-javascript. I encourage you to write the code yourself. Writing is another form of learning, and in most cases, the code you understand best is the code you wrote.

Feedback

I will be glad to hear your feedback. For comments, questions or suggestions regarding this book send me an email to cristi_salcescu@yahoo.com.

Chapter 1: A brief overview of JavaScript

JavaScript has primitives, objects and functions. All of them are values. All are treated as objects, even primitives.

Primitives

Number, boolean, string, **undefined** and **null** are primitives.

Number

At the moment there is only one number type in JavaScript, the 64-bit binary floating point. Decimal numbers' arithmetic is inexact. As you may already know, 0.1 + 0.2 does not make 0.3 . But with integers, the arithmetic is exact, so 1 + 2 === 3.

Numbers inherit methods from the Number.prototype object. Methods can be called on numbers:

```
(123).toString();  //"123"
(1.23).toFixed(1); //"1.2"
```

There are functions for converting strings to numbers:
Number.parseInt(), Number.parseFloat() and Number().

```
Number.parseInt("1");       //1
Number.parseInt("text");    //NaN
Number.parseFloat("1.234"); //1.234
Number("1");                //1
Number("1.234");            //1.234
```

Invalid arithmetic operations or invalid conversions will not throw an exception, but will result in the NaN "Not-a-Number" value. isNaN() can detect NaN .

String

A string stores a series of Unicode characters. Text can be inside double quotes "" or single quotes ''.

Strings inherit methods from String.prototype. They have methods like substring(), indexOf() or concat().

```
"text".substring(1,3); //"ex"
"text".indexOf('x');   //2
"text".concat(" end"); //"text end"
```

Strings, like all primitives, are immutable. For example concat() doesn't modify the existing string but creates a new one.

The + operator can add or concatenate:

```
1 + 1      //2
"1" + "1"  //"11"
1 + "1"    //"11"
```

Boolean

A boolean has two values: true and false.

The language has truthy and falsy values. false, null, undefined, ''(empty string), 0 and NaN are falsy. All other values are truthy.

Truthy values are evaluated to true when executed in a boolean context. Falsy values are evaluated to false. The next example displays the false branch.

```
if('') {
  console.log("true");
} else {
  console.log("false");
}
```

The equality operator is ===. The not equal operator is !== .

Variables

Variables can be defined using var, let and const.

`var` declares and optionally initializes a variable. Variables declared with `var` have function scope. They are treated as declared at the top of the function. This is called variable hoisting.

The `let` and `const` declaration have block scope. A variable declared with `const` cannot be reassigned.

The value of a variable that is not initialize is **undefined**.

Objects   *key: value*

An object is a dynamic collection of properties.

The property key is a unique string. The property value can be a primitive, an object or a function.

The simplest way to create an object is to use an object literal:

```
let obj = {
  message: "read me",
  doSomething: function() {}
}
```

There are two ways for accessing properties: the dot notation and the bracket notation. Object's properties can be read, added, edited or removed.

```
let obj = {};
obj.message = "read me"; //add
obj.message = "enjoy"; //edit
delete obj.message; //remove
```

All object's properties are public.

Primitives vs objects

Primitives, except **null** and **undefined**, are treated like objects in the sense they have methods, but they are not objects.

Numbers, strings and booleans have equivalent wrapper objects. These are built with the **Number**, **String** and **Boolean** functions.

In order to allow access to properties on primitives, JavaScript creates a wrapper object and then destroys it. The process of creating and destroying wrapper objects is optimized by the JavaScript engine.

Array

Arrays are indexed collections of values. Each value is an element. Elements are ordered and accessed by their index number.

JavaScript has array-like objects. Arrays are implemented using objects. Indexes are converted to strings and used as keys for retrieving values.

A simple array like `let arr = ['A', 'B', 'C']` is emulated using an object like the one below:

```
{
  '0': 'A',
  '1': 'B',
  '2': 'C'
}
```

Note that `arr[1]` gives the same value as `arr['1']`:

```
arr[1] === arr['1']; //true
```

Removing values from an array with `delete` will leave holes. `splice()` can be used to avoid the problem, but it can be slow.

```
let arr = ['A', 'B', 'C'];
delete arr[1];
console.log(arr); //['A', empty, 'C']
console.log(arr.length); //3
```

JavaScript's arrays don't throw "index out of range" exceptions. If the index is not available, they will return `undefined`.

Stack and queue can be easily implemented using array methods:

```
let stack = [];
stack.push(1);          //[1]
stack.push(2);          //[1, 2]
let last = stack.pop(); //[1]
console.log(last);      //2

let queue = [];
queue.push(1);          //[1]
queue.push(2);          //[1, 2]
let first = queue.shift();//[2]
console.log(first);     //1
```

Functions

Functions are independent units of behavior. There are three ways to define a function:

- Function declaration (aka function statement)
- Function expression (aka function literal)
- Arrow function

The function declaration

```
function doSomething(){ }
```

- `function` is the first keyword on the line.
- It must have a name.
- It can be used before definition. Function declarations are moved, or "hoisted", to the top of their scope.

The function expression

```
let doSomething = function() { }
```

- `function` is not the first keyword on the line.
- Name is optional. There can be anonymous function expressions or named function expressions.
- It needs to be defined, then it can execute.
- It can auto-execute after definition. It is called IIFE, Immediately Invoked Function Expression. It is also known as a self-executing function.

Here is an example of an IIFE:

```
(function autorun(){
  console.log("executed");
})();
//"executed"
```

Arrow function

The arrow function is a sugar syntax for creating an anonymous function expression.

```
let doSomething = () => { };
```

Function invocation

Functions can be invoked in different ways:

```
//as functions
doSomething(arguments);

//as methods
theObject.doSomething(arguments);

//as constructors
new Constructor(arguments)

//with apply() or call()
doSomething.apply(theObject, [arguments]);
doSomething.call(theObject, arguments);
```

Functions can be invoked with more or fewer arguments than declared in the definition. The extra arguments will be ignored, and the missing arguments will be set to **undefined**.

Functions, except arrow functions, have two pseudo-parameters: **this** and **arguments**.

this

Methods are functions that are stored in objects. In order for a function to know on which object to work on, **this** is used. **this** represents the function's context.

When functions are used as methods, **this** represents the object.

```
let theObject = {
  name: "name",
  getName: function(){
    return this.name;
  }
}
```

```
theObject.getName(); //"name"
```

When a function is used as a constructor **new Constructor()**, **this** represents the newly created object. Arrow functions can't be used as constructors.

Functions are objects, as a result functions can have methods. The
`apply()` and `call()` methods execute the function with a given `this`.
`call()` provides the arguments individually, while `apply()` accepts an
array with all arguments.

```
let otherObject = {
  name: "otherName"
}


function getName(){
  return this.name;
}


getName.apply(otherObject); //"otherName"
getName.call(otherObject);  //"otherName"
```

There is no point to use `this` when a function is invoked with the function
form. In that case `this` is `undefined` or is the `window` object, depending
if strict mode is enabled or not. Consider the next example:

```
"use strict";
function getName(){
  return this.name;
}


getName();
//Cannot read property 'name' of undefined
```

The value of `this` depends on how the function is invoked, not where the
function is defined. This is of course a source of confusion.

arguments

The `arguments` pseudo-parameter gives all the arguments used at invocation. It is an array-like object, but not an array. It lacks the array
methods.

```
function logAll(){
  console.log(arguments);
}


logAll("msg1", "msg2", "msg3");
//Arguments(3) ["msg1","msg2","msg3"]
```

return

return stops the function execution and returns the result. When it returns no value or there is no **return** at all, the function still returns **undefined**.

The automatic semi-colon insertion may create problems when using **return**. The following function will not return an empty object, but rather **undefined**.

```
function getObject(){
  return
  {
  }
}


getObject();
```

Curly brackets should be opened { on the same line as **return**.

Dynamic typing

JavaScript has dynamic typing. Values have types, variables do not. Types can change at run time.

```
function log(value){
  console.log(value);
}


log(1);
log("text");
log({message: "text"});
```

The **typeof()** operator can check the type of a variable.

```
let n = 1;
typeof(n);    //"number"

let s = "text";
typeof(s);    //"string"

let fn = function() {};
typeof(fn);   //"function"
```

Dynamic typing offers a higher flexibility.

Exceptions

JavaScript has an exception handling mechanism. It works like you may expect, by wrapping the code using the `try/catch` statement. The statement has a single `catch` block that handles all exceptions.

You can **throw** values of any type, but is common to throw error objects.

It is good to know that JavaScript sometimes has a preference for silent errors. Strict mode eliminates some of JavaScript silent errors.

Final thoughts

JavaScript allows to access properties on primitives.

Objects are dynamic collection of key-value pairs.

Arrays are indexed collections of values.

Functions are independent units and can be invoked in different ways.

Primitives, objects and functions are all values.

Chapter 2: New features in ES6+

ES6+ comes with more features. Some new syntax allows you to write code in a more expressive way, some features complete the functional programming toolbox, and some features are questionable.

let and const

There are two ways for declaring a variable, `let` and `const`, plus one that is becoming obsolete, `var`.

let

`let` declares and optionally initializes a variable in the current scope. The current scope can be either a module, a function or a block.

Scope defines the lifetime and visibility of a variable. Variables are not visible outside the scope in which they are declared.

Consider the next code that emphasizes the `let` block scope:

```
let x = 1;
{
  let x = 2;
}
console.log(x); //1
```

In contrast, the `var` declaration had no block scope:

```
var x = 1;
{
  var x = 2;
```

```
}
console.log(x); //2
```

const

`const` declares a variable that cannot be reassigned. It becomes a constant only when the assigned value is immutable.

An immutable value is a value that, once created, cannot be changed. Primitive values are immutable, objects are mutable.

The initialization of the `const` variable is mandatory.

Modules

Before modules, a variable declared outside any function was a global variable. With modules, a variable declared outside any function is hidden and not available to other modules unless it is explicitly exported.

There are two kinds of exports: default and named exports.

Let's first look at default exports and imports. Exporting makes a function or object available to other modules.

```
//module "./TodoStore.js"
export default function TodoStore(){}

//module "./UserStore.js"
export default function UserStore(){}
```

Importing makes a function or object, from other modules, available to the current module.

```
//module "./main.js"
import TodoStore from "./TodoStore";
import UserStore from "./UserStore";

const todoStore = TodoStore();
const userStore = UserStore();
```

When using the default export, the import name can by different than the export name. In the next example, the `flow` function exported as default is used with the name `pipe`.

```
import pipe from "lodash/flow";
```

Let's now look at named exports and imports. Below is an example of exporting two named functions:

```
//module "./tools.js"
export function compose(...args){}
export function decorate(f, ...args){}
```

Then, they can be imported using the same name:

```
//module "./main.js"
import { compose, decorate } from "./tools";
```

There can be one default export and many named exports per module file.

In a way, we can imagine a module as a self-executing function that takes the import data as input and returns the export data.

Spread/Rest

The ... operator can be the spread operator or the rest parameter, depending on where it is used.

The spread operator splits an object or array into individual values.

```
const numbers = [1, 2, 3];
const arr = ['a', 'b', 'c', ...numbers];

console.log(arr);
//["a", "b", "c", 1, 2, 3]
```

The rest parameter gathers the remaining arguments when the number of arguments exceeds the number of named parameters. The rest parameter is the last parameter in the function and is an array.

```
function process(x,y, ...arr){
   console.log(arr)
}

process(1, 2, 3, 4, 5);
//[3, 4, 5]

function processArray(...arr){
   console.log(arr)
}
```

```
processArray(1, 2, 3, 4, 5);
//[1, 2, 3, 4, 5]
```

Cloning

The spread operator makes cloning of objects and arrays simpler and more expressive.

```
const book = { title: "JavaScript: The Good Parts" };

//clone with Object.assign()
const clone = Object.assign({}, book);

//clone with spread operator
const clone = { ...book };

const arr = [1, 2 ,3];

//clone with slice()
const cloneArr = arr.slice();

//clone with spread operator
const cloneArr = [ ...arr ];
```

Merging objects

The spread operator, like `Object.assign()`, can be used to copy properties from one or more objects to an empty object and merge their properties.

```
const authorGateway = {
  getAuthors: function() {},
  editAuthor: function() {}
};

const bookGateway = {
  getBooks: function() {},
  editBook: function() {}
};

//copy with Object.assign()
const gateway = Object.assign({},
```

```
        authorGateway,
        bookGateway);

//copy with spread operator
const gateway = {
    ...authorGateway,
    ...bookGateway
};
```

The `gateway` object contains properties from both `authorGateway` and `bookGateway` objects. When multiple objects have a property with the same name, the property from the last object overwrites the previous ones.

Concatenating arrays

In the next example, the spread operator is used to concatenate arrays:

```
const part1 = [1, 2, 3];
const part2 = [4, 5, 6];

//concatenate with concat()
const arr = part1.concat(part2);

//concatenate with spread operator
const arr = [...part1, ...part2];

console.log(arr);
//[1, 2, 3, 4, 5, 6]
```

arguments

With the rest parameter we can replace the `arguments` pseudo-parameter. The rest parameter is an array, `arguments` is not.

```
function logAll(...args){
    console.log(args);
}

logAll("msg1", "msg2", "msg3");
//["msg1", "msg2", "msg3"]
```

Property short-hands

Consider the next code:

```
function BookGateway(){
  function getBooks() {}
  function editBook() {}

  return {
    getBooks: getBooks,
    editBook: editBook
  }
}
```

With property short-hands, when the property name and the name of the variable used as value are the same, we can just write the key once.

```
function BookGateway(){
  function getBooks() {}
  function editBook() {}

  return {
    getBooks,
    editBook
  }
}
```

Here is another example:

```
const todoStore = TodoStore();
const userStore = UserStore();

const stores = {
  todoStore,
  userStore
};
```

Destructuring assignment

The destructuring assignment syntax extracts values from objects or arrays into variables.

Consider the next code:

```
function TodoStore(args){
  const helper = args.helper;
  const dataAccess = args.dataAccess;
  const userStore = args.userStore;
}
```

With the destructuring assignment syntax, it can be written like this:

```
function TodoStore(args){
  const {
    helper,
    dataAccess,
    userStore } = args;
}
```

The destructuring syntax can be used directly in the parameter list:

```
function TodoStore({helper, dataAccess, userStore}){}
```

Here is the function call:

```
TodoStore({
  helper: {},
  dataAccess: {},
  userStore: {}
});
```

Default parameters

Functions can have default parameters. Look at the next example:

```
function log(message, mode = "Info"){
  console.log(mode + ": " + message);
}

log("An info");
//Info: An info

log("An error", "Error");
//Error: An error
```

Template string literals

Template strings are defined with the ' character. With template strings, the previous logging message can be written like this:

```
function log(message, mode= "Info"){
  console.log(`${mode}: ${message}`);
}
```

Template strings can be defined on multiple lines. However, a better option is to keep the long text messages as resources.

See below a function generating an HTML that spans multiple lines:

```
function createTodoItemHtml(todo){
  return `<li>
    <div>${todo.title}</div>
    <div>${todo.userName}</div>
  </li>`;
}
```

Class

Class is sugar syntax for creating objects with a custom prototype. It has a better syntax than the previous one, the function constructor. Take a look at the next example:

```
class Service {
  doSomething(){
    console.log("do-something");
  }
}

const service = new Service();
console.log(service.__proto__ === Service.prototype);
```

All methods defined in the `Service` class will be added to the `Service.prototype` object. Instances of the `Service` class will have the same prototype object, `Service.prototype`. All instances will delegate method calls to the prototype object. Methods are defined once in the prototype and then inherited by all instances.

Inheritance

"Classes can inherit from other classes". Below is an example of inheritance where the `SpecialService` class "inherits" from the `Service` class:

```
class Service {
  doSomething(){
    console.log("do-something");
  }
}

class SpecialService extends Service {
  doSomethingElse(){
    console.log("do-something-else");
  }
}

const specialService = new SpecialService();
specialService.doSomething();
specialService.doSomethingElse();
```

All methods defined in the `SpecialService` class will be added to the `SpecialService.prototype` object. All instances will delegate method calls to the `SpecialService.prototype` object. If the method is not found in `SpecialService.prototype` it will be searched in the `Service.prototype` object. If it is still not found it will be searched in `Object.prototype`.

Arrow functions

Arrow functions can create anonymous functions on the fly. They can be used to create small callbacks, with a shorter syntax.

Consider the next code selecting only the `title` from a collection of to-dos:

```
const todos = [
  {id: 1, title: "learn", type:"NC", completed: false},
  {id: 2, title: "connect", type:"RC", completed: true}
];

const titles = todos.map(todo => todo.title);
//["learn", "connect"]
```

Here is an example selecting the to-dos that are not completed:

```
const filteredTodos = todos.filter(todo => !todo.completed);
//{id: 1, title: "learn", type: "NC", completed: false}
```

Below is an example of the same function written with the function declaration and the arrow syntax:

```
function isNewContent(todo){
    return todo.type === "NC";
}


const isNewContent = todo => todo.type === "NC";
```

this

Arrow functions don't have their own **this** and **arguments**. Arrow function can't be used as constructor functions.

Using **bind()**, **apply()** or **call()** to set the value of **this** on an arrow function has no effect. Consider the code below:

```
this.message = "help";

const logMessage = ()=>{
  console.log(this.message);
}

logMessage(); //"help"
logMessage.call({message : "identify"}); //"help"
```

this and **arguments** are treated like any other free variables used in the function definition.

Proper tail-calls

> A recursive function is tail recursive when the recursive call is the last thing the function does.

The tail recursive functions perform better than non tail recursive functions. The optimized tail recursive call does not create a new stack frame for each function call, but rather uses a single stack frame.

ES6 brings the tail-call optimization in strict mode.

The following function should benefit from the tail-call optimization:

```
function print(from, to)
{
  const n = from;
  if (n > to)  return;

  console.log(n);

//last statement is the recursive call
  print(n + 1, to);
}

print(1, 3);
//1
//2
//3
```

Note that the tail-call optimization is not yet supported by major browsers.

Promises

> A promise is an object that represents a possible future result
> of an asynchronous operation.

A promise can be in one of the three states: pending, resolved or rejected. The promise will be in pending until is either resolved or rejected.

Creating a promise

Let's create a delay() function using a Promise:

```
function delay(duration){
  return new Promise(function(resolve, reject){
    setTimeout(resolve, duration);
  });
}

function logMessage(){
  console.log("process ended");
}

delay(5000)
  .then(logMessage);
```

The `Promise` constructor takes as single argument, a function called "the executor function". This function is executed immediately when the promise is created.

The executor function takes two callbacks: `resolve` and `reject`.

- Calling `resolve()` resolves the promise.
- Calling `reject()` rejects the promise.

Both functions can be called with one argument. The promise is resolved or rejected only once. Any future invocations of these methods have no effect.

Using a promise

After making a promise, callbacks can be registered. They will be called when the promise result is known.

```
function fetchUsers(){
  return fetch("/users");
}

function doSomething(){ }
function handleError(error){ }

fetchUsers()
  .then(doSomething)
  .catch(handleError);
```

`doSomething()` is called when promise is resolved. `handleError()` is called when promise is rejected. `doSomething()` doesn't need to return a promise.

`then()` can handle both success and fail, but it is clearer to handle success with it and handle rejection with `catch()`.

Final thoughts

`let` and `const` declare and initialize variables.

Modules encapsulate functionality and expose only a small part.

The spread operator, rest parameter and property shorthand make things easier to express.

Promises and tail recursion complete the functional programming toolbox.

Chapter 3: First-class functions

The best thing about JavaScript is its implementation of functions.— Douglas Crockford, author of JavaScript The Good Parts

First-class functions

JavaScript has first-class functions. It means that functions can be used as any other values. Numbers and functions are both values, so we can use a function in a similar way we use a number:

- Numbers can be stored in variables → functions can be store in variables. In fact functions can be stored in variables, objects or arrays.
- Numbers can be passed as arguments to functions → functions can be passed as arguments to other functions
- Functions can return numbers → functions can return other functions

See the next examples:

```
//store in variable
function doSomething(){ }
```

```
//store in variable
const doSomething = function (){ };
```

```
//store in property
const obj = {
   doSomething : function(){ }
}
```

```
//pass as argument
process(doSomething);

//return from function
function createGenerator(){
  return function(){
  }
}
```

Function names are treated like variables. In essence, the function declaration syntax creates a variable that keeps a function:

```
//function declaration syntax
function doSomething() {}

//is equivalent to
let doSomething = function() {}
```

Higher-order functions

A higher-order function is a function that takes another function as argument, returns a function or does both.

Let's built the `doWithLoading(fn)` higher-order function that takes a function **fn** as argument and executes it. It displays a loading message before and after the input function execution.

```
function doWithLoading(fn){
  console.log("start loading");
  const returnValue = fn();
  console.log("end loading");
  return returnValue;
}

function process() {
  console.log("process");
}

doWithLoading(process);
//start loading
//process
//end loading
```

Working with arrays in a functional style involves using a set of built-in higher-order functions: `filter()`, `map()` and `reduce()`.

filter()

> `filter()` selects values from a list using a predicate function that decides what values to keep.

```
const numbers = [1,2,3,4,5,6];

function isEven(number){
  return number % 2 === 0;
}

const evenNumbers = numbers.filter(isEven);
//element=1, isEven(1) is false → result=[]
//element=2, isEven(2) is true  → result=[2]
//element=3, isEven(3) is false → result=[2]
//element=4, isEven(4) is true  → result=[2, 4]
//element=5, isEven(5) is false → result=[2, 4]
//element=6, isEven(6) is true  → result=[2, 4, 6]
//[2, 4, 6]
```

> A predicate function is a function that takes one argument and returns **true** or **false**. It tests if the input value satisfies the condition.

> A callback is a function passed as an argument to another function.

`isEven()` is a predicate function and is used as a callback.

map()

> `map()` transforms a list of values to another list of values using a mapping function.

```
function toCodeOfLength(number){
  return "a".repeat(number);
}

const numbers = [1, 2, 3];
const codes = numbers.map(toCodeOfLength);
```

```
//element=1, map to "a"    → result=["a"]
//element=2, map to "aa"   → result=["a", "aa"]
//element=3, map to "aaa"  → result=["a", "aa", "aaa"]
//["a", "aa", "aaa"]
```

toCodeOfLength() is a mapping function. It takes a value and computes another value.

reduce()

reduce() reduces a list of values to one value using a reducer function.

The reducer function takes the accumulator value and the current value and computes the new accumulator value. The reduce() method executes the reducer function for each element in the array.

```
function addNumber(total, number){
  return total + number;
}

const numbers = [1, 2, 3];
const total = numbers.reduce(addNumber, 0);
//element=1, total=0 → result=1
//element=2, total=1 → result=3
//element=3, total=3 → result=6
//6
```

addNumber() is a reducer function.

reduce(reducer, initialValue) takes a second argument as the initial value for the accumulator. If no value is provided, it sets the first element in the array as the initial value and starts the loop from the second element.

```
const numbers = [1, 2, 3];
const total = numbers.reduce(addNumber);
//element=2, total=1 → result=3
//element=3, total=3 → result=6
//6
```

There is also a reduceRight() method that starts from the last element in the list.

```
function multiply(product, value){
  return product * value;
}


const numbers = [2, 3, 4];
const product = numbers.reduceRight(multiply, 1);
//element=4, product=1  → result=4
//element=3, product=4  → result=12
//element=2, product=12 → result=24
//24
```

As you note, when multiplying the initial value for the accumulator is 1.

sort()

> sort() sorts the elements of the array using a comparison function. It is an impure method, it modifies the input array.
>
> The comparison function takes two arguments, a and b for example, and returns negative, positive or zero. When result is negative then a comes before b. When it is positive a comes after b. When it is zero, a and b are not sorted in regards to each other.

```
function asc(a, b){
  return a - b;
}


function desc(a, b){
  return b - a;
}


const numbers = [1,3,2,6,4,5];


numbers.sort(asc);
//[1, 2, 3, 4, 5, 6]


numbers.sort(desc);
//[6, 5, 4, 3, 2, 1]
```

asc() and desc() are comparison functions. Given the same input the comparison function should always return the same output.

Extended toolbox

find() returns the first value that satisfies the predicate function. It stops processing when it finds the first value.

findIndex() returns the index of the first value that satisfies the predicate function.

some() checks if at least one value in the list passes the test implemented by the predicate function. It stops processing when the predicate returns true.

every() checks if all values in the list pass the test implemented by the predicate function. It stops processing when the predicate returns false.

Let's use them:

```
const numbers = [1,2,3,4,5,6];

const firstEven = numbers.find(isEven);
//2

const firstEvenIndex = numbers.findIndex(isEven);
//1

const areAllEven = numbers.every(isEven);
//false

const hasOneEven = numbers.some(isEven);
//true
```

forEach() calls the callback function for each element in an array, in order.

```
function log(value){
  console.log(value);
}

const numbers = [1,2,3];
numbers.forEach(log);
//1
//2
//3
```

All these array methods are built-in higher-order functions.

Final thoughts

Having first-class functions is the ability to use functions as values. It makes it easy to pass around behavior and work with functions like with any other values.

`filter()`, `map()`, `reduce()` make the basic toolbox for working with collections in a functional style.

Chapter 4: Closures

Closure is an inner function that has access to the outer scope, even after the outer scope container has executed.

Scope defines the lifetime and visibility of a variable. The outer scope container can be a function, a block or a module.

Nested functions

Functions can be nested inside other functions. Consider the next code:

```
(function autorun(){
    let x = 1;
    function log(){
        console.log(x);
    }
    log();
})();
```

`log()` is a nested function. `log()` accesses variable x from its outer scope. The `log()` function is a closure. The outer scope container is the outer function.

The inner function accessing variables from the outer function is a closure.

Lexical scope

Lexical scope is the ability of the inner function to access the outer scope in which it is defined. Consider the next code:

```
(function autorun(){
    let x = 1;
    function log(){
      console.log(x);
```

```
    };

    function run(fn){
        let x = 100;
        fn();
    }

    run(log); //1
})();
```

The log() function is a closure. It refers the x variable from its parent function autorun(). log() doesn't use the x variable from the run() function.

The closure function has access to the scope in which it is created, not the scope in which it is executed.

The local function scope of autorun() is the lexical scope of the log() function.

Surviving parent execution

Closure becomes important when the inner function survives the execution of the parent scope container. This happens in the following situations:

- The inner function is used as a callback for an asynchronous task like a timer, an event or a network call
- The parent function or module returns the inner function or returns an object storing the inner function

Consider the next examples:

Timer

```
(function autorun(){
    let x = 1;
    setTimeout(function log(){
        console.log(x);
    }, 10000);
})();
```

The x variable lives until the log() function invocation.

If `setInterval()` had been used, the x variable would have lived forever or until `clearInterval()` was called.

Event

```
(function autorun(){
  let x = 1;
  $("#btn").click(function log(){
    console.log(x);
  });
})();
```

When the variable x is used in an event handler, it lives forever or until the handler is removed.

Network call

```
(function autorun(){
  let x = 1;
  fetch("/todos").then(function log(){
    console.log(x);
  });
})();
```

The x variable lives until the response gets back from the Web API and the callback is executed.

In all these cases, `log()` is a closure and survives the invocation of the parent function.

The variable lifetime depends on the closure lifetime. Variables live as long as the closure referring them lives. If a variable is shared by many closures, all closures should be garbage collected before the variable is garbage collected.

Closures in loop

Closures store references to outer variables, they don't copy the actual values. Check the next example:

```
function initEvents(){
  for(var i=1; i<=3; i++){
    $("#btn"+i).click(function log(){
      console.log(i); //4
```

```
    });
  }
}
```

initEvents();

In this example, three closures were created, all sharing the same i variable. All three closures are event handlers. Because i changes during the loop, all logs will display the same value, the last one.

The simplest way to fix this issue is to use the for statement with a let declaration inside. It will create a variable local to the block scope for each iteration.

```
function initEvents(){
  for(let i=1; i<=3; i++){
    $("#btn"+i).click(function log(){
      console.log(i); //1 2 3
    });
  }
}
```

initEvents();

When the variable declaration is done outside the for statement, even if it is done with let, all closures will use the same variable. All logs will display the same value, the last one.

```
function initEvents(){
  let i;
  for(i=1; i<=3; i++){
    $("#btn"+i).click(function log(){
      console.log(i); //4
    });
  }
}
```

initEvents();

Generators

A generator is a function that returns the next value from the sequence each time it is called.

I think the ES6 generator is an unnecessary feature that makes code more complicated.

The ES6 generator creates an object that has the **next()** method. The **next()** method creates an object that has the **value** property. ES6 generators promote the use of loops and in functional programming we want to get away from loops.

Consider the ES6 generator below:

```
function* sequence(){
  let count = 0;
  while(true) {
    count += 1;
    yield count;
  }
}

const generator = sequence();
generator.next().value; //1
generator.next().value; //2
generator.next().value; //3
```

The same generator can be simply implemented with a closure:

```
function sequence(){
  let count = 0;
  return function(){
    count += 1;
    return count;
  }
}

const generator = sequence();
generator(); //1
generator(); //2
generator(); //3
```

The **generator()** function is a closure. It has access to the **count** variable from its parent **sequence()**. It can access the **count** variable even after **sequence()** is executed.

The **generator()** closure is created using a function that returns a function. This way the closure function survives the invocation of its parent. **sequence()** is a higher-order function.

Function with private state

With closures, we can create functions with private state. Closures encapsulate state.

The **generator()** closure is a function with private state. Each time it is called, it remembers its previous **count** state and returns the next consecutive number. The **count** variable is private, there is no access to it from the outside.

Functions with private state

We can take this idea further and create more closures sharing the same private state. In the next example, **increment()** and **decrement()** are two closures sharing the same private **state** variable.

```
const counter = (function(){
    let state = 0;

    function increment(){
        state += 1;
        return state;
    }

    function decrement(){
        state -= 1;
        return state;
    }

    return {
        increment,
        decrement
    }
})();

counter.increment(); //1
counter.increment(); //2
counter.decrement(); //1
```

This practice is known as the Revealing Module pattern.

The same behavior can be achieved using ES6 modules.

```
//module "./counter.js"
```

```
let state = 0;

function increment() {
   state += 1;
   return state;
}

function decrement() {
   state -= 1;
   return state;
}

export default {
   increment,
   decrement
}

//module "./index.js"
import counter from "./counter";

counter.increment(); //1
counter.increment(); //2
counter.decrement(); //1
```

Scope objects

When a function is executed a new private scope object is created. The scope object contains all the arguments and local variables. It also contains a reference to the scope object of the outer scope where it was created.

Scope objects are allocated like any other objects. Scope objects are not automatically cleaned up after the function execution. They are garbage collected like ordinary objects when there are no more references to them.

Scope objects make a scope chain. It is similar in concept to the prototype chain. When a variable is used, the program looks down the scope chain until it finds that variable.

A closure is a function having a private reference to the scope object of the outer "function" where it is created.

Garbage collection

The private state of a closure becomes eligible for garbage collection after the closure itself is garbage collected. To make this possible, the closure should no longer have a reference to it.

In the next example, first the `add()` closure function is created:

```
let add = (function createAddClosure(){
    let arr = [];
    return function(obj){
        arr.push(obj);
    }
})();
```

Then, two functions working with the closure function are defined:

- `addALotOfObjects()` adds a lot of objects to the closure's private state.
- `clearAllObjects()` sets the closure reference to `null`.

Both functions are used as event handlers:

```
function Todo(){}

function addALotOfObjects(){
    for(let i=1; i<=10000;i++) {
        add(new Todo(i));
    }
}

function clearAllObjects(){
    if(add){
        add = null;
    }
}

$("#add").click(addALotOfObjects);
$("#clear").click(clearAllObjects);
```

Clicking "Add" will add 10,000 to-dos to the closure's private state.

Constructor	# New	# Deleted	# Delta	Alloc. Size	Freed Size	Size Delta
▶ Todo	10 000	0	+10 000	320 000	0	+320 000

Clicking "Clear" will set the closure reference to **null**. After doing that, the private state is garbage collected.

Constructor	# New	# Deleted ▼	# Delta	Alloc. Size	Freed Size	Size Delta
▶ Todo	0	10 000	−10 000	0	320 000	−320 000

Final thoughts

Closures are inner functions having access to variables from the outer scopes.

Variables used in closures live as long as closures live.

Closures create encapsulation.

First-class functions and closures open the way for functional programming in JavaScript.

Chapter 5: Function decorators

> A function decorator is a higher-order function that takes one function as an argument and returns another function, and the returned function is a variation of the argument function.— Reginald Braithwaite, author of JavaScript Allongé

In order to see the concept in practice, we will write some common function decorators found in libraries like lodash.js, underscore.js or ramda.js.

once()

once(fn) creates a function that executes the original function only one time. It is useful when we want to execute the function once, no matter how many times is called from different places.

```
function once(fn){
  let returnValue;
  let canRun = true;
  return function(...args){
    if(canRun) {
        returnValue = fn(...args);
        canRun = false;
    }
    return returnValue;
  }
}

function process(){
  console.log("process");
```

```
}
```

```
const processOnce = once(process);
processOnce(); //process
processOnce(); //
processOnce(); //
```

once() is a function that returns another function. The returned function is a closure. Note how the original function is called with all the arguments: fn(...args).

after()

after(fn, count) creates a version of the function that executes only after a number of calls. For example, it can be used to run the function after all asynchronous operations have finished.

```
function after(fn, startCount){
  let count = 0;
  return function(...args){
    count = count + 1;
    if (count >= startCount) {
        return fn(...args);
    }
  }
}
```

```
function logResult() {
  console.log("finish");
}
```

```
const logResultAfter2 = after(logResult, 2);
setTimeout(function firstCall(){
  console.log("1st");
  logResultAfter2();
}, 3000);
```

```
setTimeout(function secondCall(){
  console.log("2nd");
  logResultAfter2();
}, 4000);
```

```
//"1st"
//"2nd"
//"finish"
```

In this example, I am using `after()` to build a new function `logResultAfter2()` that executes the original code of `logResult()` starting with the second call.

throttle()

`throttle(fn, wait)` creates a version of the function that, when invoked repeatedly, will call the original function once per every `wait` milliseconds. It is useful for limiting events that occur faster.

```
function throttle(fn, interval) {
  let lastTime;
  return function throttled(...args) {
    if(!lastTime || (Date.now() - lastTime >= interval)) {
      fn(...args);
      lastTime = Date.now();
    }
  }
}
```

```
let throttledProcess = throttle(process, 1000);
$(window).mousemove(throttledProcess);
```

In this example, moving the mouse will generate a lot of `mousemove` events, but the original function will be called once per second.

debounce()

`debounce(fn, wait)` creates a version of the function that, when invoked repeatedly, will call the original function after `wait` milliseconds since the last invocation. It is useful for running a function only after the event has stopped arriving.

```
function debounce(fn, interval) {
  let timer;
  return function debounced(...args) {
    clearTimeout(timer);
    timer = setTimeout(function(){
      fn(...args);
```

```
    }, interval);
  }
}
```

```
let debouncedProcess = debounce(process, 400);
$(window).resize(debouncedProcess);
```

Some common events to take in consideration for **debounce** are **scroll**, **resize**, **mousemove** or **keypress**.

memoize()

Memoization is a technique for improving execution speed by saving the previous results and use them to avoid computation. Memoization is different than caching, in the sense that it works only with deterministic functions.

memoize(fn) creates a memoized version of a function. It is useful for speeding up slow computations.

Here is an implementation taking a function with one argument.

```
function memoize(fn) {
  const map = Object.create(null);
  return function (x) {
    if (!map[x]){
      map[x] = fn(x);
    }

    return map[x];
  }
}
```

```
const factorial = memoize(function(n){
  console.log("n=" + n);
  if(n < 2) return 1;
  return n * factorial(n-1);
});
```

```
console.log(factorial(3)); //6;
//n=3
//n=2
//n=1
```

```
console.log(factorial(5)); //120;
//n=5
//n=4
```

`factorial()` is a function with private state. The internal state is a map storing the previous results.

unary()

`unary(fn)` creates a version of the function that takes only one argument. It is usually used to fix problems when the function is called with more arguments than necessary.

```
function unary(fn){
  return function(first){
    return fn(first);
  }
}
```

Let's try to use `console.log()` to log all numbers from an array.

```
const numbers = [1,2,3,4,5,6];
```

```
numbers.forEach(console.log);
//1 0 (6) [1, 2, 3, 4, 5, 6]
//2 1 (6) [1, 2, 3, 4, 5, 6]
//...
```

As you can see, there is a problem. `console.log()` receives more arguments than we want. We need to call it with only one argument. Here is the code using the `unary()` function:

```
numbers.forEach(unary(console.log));
//1 2 3 4 5 6
```

Below is another example using `unary()` to fix problems with `parseInt()`:

```
const numbers = ['1','2','3','4','5','6'];
```

```
numbers.map(parseInt);
//[1, NaN, NaN, NaN, NaN, NaN]
```

```
numbers.map(unary(parseInt));
//[1, 2, 3, 4, 5, 6]
```

binary()

binary(fn) creates a version of the function that takes only two arguments. It can be used to fix problems when the function is called with more than two arguments.

```
function binary(fn){
  return function(a, b){
    return fn(a, b);
  }
}
```

In the next example, Math.max() is called with more arguments than we may expect. Because one of the arguments, the forth, cannot be converted to a number the result is NaN.

```
const numbers = [1, 2, 3];
numbers.reduce(Math.max);
//NaN
```

To make sure Math.max() is called with two arguments we can use the binary() decorator:

```
const numbers = [1, 2, 3];
numbers.reduce(binary(Math.max));
//3

numbers.reduce(binary(Math.min));
//1
```

Preserve function context

In order to preserve the original function context we need to do two things:

- The decorator should return a function using the function keyword, not the arrow syntax.
- The original function should be called with fn.apply(this, args) or fn.call(this, ...args).

Final thoughts

Function decorators are a powerful tool for creating variations of existing functions without modifying the original functions. They can be part of the functional programming toolbox for reusing common logic.

Chapter 6: Pure functions

A pure function is a function that given the same input always returns the same output and has no side effects.

Pure functions promise to make code easier to read, understand, test, debug, compose. These are big promises. Let's see what they can do.

Reading from inside

We don't need to think how changing the value of a variable in the current function will affect other functions. We don't need to think how changing the value of a variable in other functions will affect the current function.

Here is a pure function:

```
function capitalize(name) {
  if(name){
    return name.charAt(0).toUpperCase() + name.slice(1);
  }

  return name;
}

capitalize("chapter");
//"Chapter"
```

When reading a pure function we can focus in one place, the current function. Pure functions give the reader less code to read.

Reading from outside

Look at the code below:

```
const arr = [1, 2, 3];
```

```
const newValue = compute(arr);

console.log(arr);
//[1, 2, 3]
```

When `compute()` is a pure function, we are sure that `console` will log [1, 2, 3], we don't need to read and understand the `compute()` function.

Less things to read and understand makes code easier to read.

Side effects

A side effect is a change of a variable from outside the local environment or an interaction with the outside environment that happens during the computation of the result.

Here are some examples of side effects:

- reading and changing state out of local scope
- modifying objects taken as arguments
- network calls
- reading and writing to DOM
- writing to console
- emitting/dispatching events
- reading and writing to local storage
- using timers

Changing the outside environment in any way is a side effect.

Mutating external state may create unexpected issues in some other distant part of the code. Especially changing input values can create hard to understand bugs. We don't know where the input object comes from or how changing it will affect other functions.

The result of a function with side effects depends on the external environment. Given the same input it may return different results as the outside state may change.

Here are a few functions with side effects:

`getNextValue()` is not pure, it changes state outside the function scope

```
let startValue = 0;

function getNextValue(){
```

```
    startValue += 1;
    return startValue;
}

getNextValue(); //1
getNextValue(); //2
```

addValue() is not pure, it mutates the input variable.

```
function addValue(list, value){
    list.push(value);
}

const numbers = [];

addValue(numbers, 1);
console.log(numbers);
//[1]

addValue(numbers, 2);
console.log(numbers);
//[1, 2]
```

Free variables

> A free variable is a variable used in a function that is neither a local variables nor a parameter of the function.

Pure functions can access free variables if they are constants. A constant is a variable declared with **const** and storing an immutable value.

```
const vatTax = 20;

function getFinalPrice(price){
  return price * (1 + vatTax/100);
}

getFinalPrice(10);
//12
```

getFinalPrice() is a pure function.

Pure functions don't access variables from the outside environment that can change.

Immutability

An immutable value is a value that, once created, cannot be changed.

Pure functions treat input values as immutable. Ideally input values should be immutable values. It is a good practice to return an immutable value.

`this` in pure functions

`this` is an implicit input.

When `this` is used, we need to use the function as a method or call the function with `call()` or `apply()` and pass in the context object.

`this` should be treated as an immutable input value, even if it is not. For example `filter()`, `map()` and `reduce()` are pure array methods, creating new arrays and using `this` as their input. `sort()` array method is impure, it modifies the input array.

When `this` is used and we invoke the function with the function form, we create a side effect. In this case, the function may give different results depending on the environment in which it is run. `this` becomes a free variable.

We want explicit inputs on functions. If we want to compose functions easily, `this` should not be used.

Making the context object explicit means to add it to the parameter list.

```
function transform(context) { }
```

I would say to avoid `this` in pure functions.

Deterministic function

A pure function is deterministic function. For a specific input it always returns the same output.

`Math.random()` or `Date.now()` will not be used in pure functions as they give different results on each call.

The next function has no side effects, but it is not deterministic. It is not a pure function:

```
function getNextValue(){
    return Math.random();
```

```
}
```

Referential transparency

> An function has referential transparency if it can be replaced
> with its output value and the application behavior doesn't
> change.

Because we can replace the function with its result it means that the
function has no side effects. A referentially transparent function does
nothing else but computing the result.

A function that has referential transparency is a pure function.

Using other pure functions

Pure functions can use other pure functions. Check the code below where
the getMaxId() pure function uses other two pure functions: prop() and
Math.max(). The addTodo() pure function uses the getMaxId() pure
function.

```
import prop from "lodash/property";

function addTodo(todos, todo) {
  const id = getMaxId(todos) + 1;
  const newTodo = { ...todo, id };
  return todos.concat([newTodo]);
}

function getMaxId(todos) {
  if(todos.length){
    const ids = todos.map(prop("id"));
    return Math.max(...ids);
  }
  return 0;
}

const todos = [];
const newTodos = addTodo(todos, { title: "improve" });

console.log(newTodos);
//[{title: "improve", id: 1}]
```

Using other impure functions

Pure functions don't invoke other impure functions with an exception. Pure functions can invoke impure functions if those impure functions only modify the input parameters and the overall purity is not affected. Consider the next code:

```
function applySort(arr){
  return arr.sort();
}

function sort(arr){
  const newArr = [...arr];
  return applySort(newArr);
}

const numbers = [3, 2, 1];
const sortedNumbers = sort(numbers);

console.log(numbers);
//[3, 2, 1];
console.log(sortedNumbers);
//[1, 2, 3]
```

applySort() is an impure function, it modifies the input array. sort() is a pure function even if it uses the impure applySort() function.

Returning a reference to an impure function doesn't affect the function purity.

Consider the next example where doImpureTask() is an impure function:

```
function doImpureTask(){}

function runFunction(){
  return doImpureTask();
}

function getFunction(){
  return doImpureTask;
}
```

runFunction() is impure. getFunction() is pure.

Purity from the inside

We can start writing code in pure functional style by just removing features:

- No use of assignment operators.
- No use of `let`, `var` statements.
- Declare variable only with `const`.
- No use of `++` or `--` update operators.
- No use of `delete`.
- No use of a variable as the first argument for `Object.assign()`.
- No use of loops.
- Use only the pure array methods.

In a pure functional style loops are replaced by pure array methods like `filter()`, `map()` or `reduce()` or by recursion.

Note that replacing all loops with recursion is practical when the engine does the tail-call optimization. At this moment, the tail-call optimization is not supported by major browsers.

Purity from the outside

Writing code in a pure functional style makes it pure both from the inside and outside.

Nevertheless, according to the definition, the purity of a function is decided from the outside, not from the inside. Look at the next function, creating a map by id from a collection:

```
function createMapById(list){
  const map = Object.create(null);
  list.forEach(function addToMap(item){
    map[item.id] = item;
  });
  return Object.freeze(map);
}

const arr = [
  { id:1, name:"mango" },
  { id:2, name:"apple" }
];
```

```
const map = createMapById(arr);
console.log(map);
//{
// 1: {id: 1, name: "mango"},
// 2: {id: 2, name: "apple"}
//}
```

The `createMapById()` is not written in a pure functional style. It uses the assignment operator and the `forEach()` impure method. However, when we look at the function from the outside, it is pure.

Purity inside a function is something to aspire to in the pursuit of clear code. The following implementations of the `getEvens()` function are both pure, but we should favor the first one:

```
function isEven(number){
  return number % 2 === 0;
}

function getEvens(numbers) {
  return numbers.filter(isEven);
}

function getEvens(numbers) {
  const evenNumbers = []
  numbers.forEach(function(number){
    if (isEven(number)) {
      evenNumbers.push(number);
    }
  });
  return evenNumbers;
}
```

The problem

The problem with pure functions is that we can't write the whole application using pure functions. There is state change, there is user interface rendering, there are user interactions, there are network calls. All these cannot be implemented with pure functions. Pure functions don't communicate with the external environment.

What can we do then? We want all the benefits of pure functions, but at the same time we cannot use 100% pure functions to do a practical application.

The benefits of pure functions are significant and we should write as many pure functions as we can. At the same time we need impure code to communicate with the environment.

I suggest to aim for purity and encapsulate impure code.

Impure code

Side effects are a common source of bugs because they make code harder to read and reason about.

Side effects can make code hard to understand, but they are necessary.

Our best approach is to encapsulate side effects. Objects are useful for encapsulating side effects.

Collecting the impure code together will make it easier to investigate these parts when bugs arise. By isolating side effects we know where to look for unexpected issues.

The goal is not only to encapsulate, but to reduce the possible kinds of side effects in a function.

Final thoughts

Taking all these in consideration, it becomes clear that pure functions make code easier to read and understand. Nevertheless, we should not lose the importance of making pure functions small, do one thing and have intention revealing names.

We should aim for purity as much as we can and encapsulate side effects. The purpose is to have a big percent of code pure and a low percent impure. This way we end up with a bigger part of the code that is easier to reason about and less code that can cause problems.

The more pure code the better.

Chapter 7: Immutability

> An immutable value is a value that, once created, cannot be changed.

Imagine you are waiting in queue. At entrance you got an electronic device showing your number. Just before you were very close to be served, your order number has changed on the screen. As you ask around why it happened, you understand that anyone in the building can change your number, but nobody knows who. While you are waiting, the order number continues to change, again and again. You now face the task of asking everyone in the building to stop changing your order number.

Back to code, imagine the order device as an `order` object with the `number` property. Imagine that the `order.number` property can be changed by any piece of code in the application. Detecting what part of the code did the change is hard. You may need to check all code that uses the `order` object and imagine how it may happened.

An immutable order object will not have this kind of problems.

Immutability in general avoids a series of unexpected bugs hard to detect and reason about.

Primitives

Primitive values are immutable, objects are not.

The best example of a immutable primitive is string. Any modification to a string will result in a new string. Consider the next examples:

```
"ABCD".substring(1,3); //"BC"
"AB" + "CD";            //"ABCD"
"AB".concat("CD");      //"ABCD"
```

In all these cases new strings are created.

Reading code

Take a look at the next code:

```
const arr = [1, 2, 3];
doSomething(arr);

console.log(arr);
//[1, 2, 3] ?
```

Can we easily say that log() will print [1, 2, 3] to console? No, we cannot. The array is a mutable data structure. It can change in the doSomething() function. We need to read and understand the doSomething() function in order to say what will be logged to console.

Here is an example of a doSomething() function that changes the array.

```
function doSomething(arr){
  arr.push(4);
}
```

If array was an immutable data structure, we could say what will be logged to the console without reading the doSomething() function. There will be less code to read and understand.

Constant

const declares a variable that cannot be reassigned. It becomes a constant only when the assigned value is immutable.

In short, using const with a primitive value defines a constant. Using const with an object value doesn't necessarily define a constant.

```
const book = {
  title : "How JavaScript Works",
  author : "Douglas Crockford"
};

book.title = "JavaScript The Good Parts";

console.log(book);
//{title: "JavaScript The Good Parts",
```

```
// author: "Douglas Crockford"}
```

Freezing objects

Freezing objects makes them immutable.

`Object.freeze()` can be used to freeze objects. Properties can't be added, deleted or changed.

```
const book = Object.freeze({
  title : "Functional-Light JavaScript",
  author : "Kyle Simpson"
});
```

```
book.title = "You Don't Know JS";
//Cannot assign to read only property 'title'
```

`Object.freeze()` does a shallow freeze. The nested objects can be changed. For deep freeze we need to recursively freeze each property of type object. Here is a `deepFreeze()` implementation:

```
function deepFreeze(object) {
  Object.keys(object).forEach(function(name){
    const value = object[name];
    if(typeof value === "object") {
      deepFreeze(value);
    }
  });
  return Object.freeze(object);
}
```

`deepFreeze()` makes plain objects immutable.

Working with immutable objects

Consider `book` as an immutable object.

```
const book = Object.freeze({
  title : "JavaScript The Good Parts",
  author : "Douglas Crockford"
});
```

Any change will require to create a new object.

Edit property

```
const title = "How JavaScript Works";
const newBook = Object.freeze({ ...book, title });

console.log(book);
//{title: "JavaScript The Good Parts",
// author: "Douglas Crockford"}

console.log(newBook);
//{title: "How JavaScript Works",
// author: "Douglas Crockford"}
```

Add property

```
const description = "Looking at the fundamentals";
const newBook = Object.freeze({ ...book, description});

console.log(book);
//{title: "JavaScript The Good Parts",
// author: "Douglas Crockford"}

console.log(newBook);
//{title: "JavaScript The Good Parts",
// author: "Douglas Crockford"}
// description: "Looking at the fundamentals"}
```

Remove property

The destructuring syntax can be used to create a new object without the author property:

```
const { author, ...newBook } = book;

console.log(book);
//{title: "JavaScript The Good Parts",
// author: "Douglas Crockford"}

console.log(newBook);
//{title: "JavaScript The Good Parts"}
```

Working with immutable arrays

The array data structure is mutable. It can be modified after it is created.

In order to work with immutable arrays we need to freeze them at creation and use mainly the pure array methods and the spread operator.

The pure array methods don't modify the existing array but create new values.

concat(), every(), filter(), find(), findIndex(), map(), reduce(), reduceRight(), slice(), some() are pure.

reverse(), sort() should be pure, but they are not. To use them, we must first make a copy of the original array.

The impure methods modify the input array.

pop(), push(), shift(), splice(), unshift() are not pure.

Object.freeze() freezes the array. Only the pure methods work.

```
const books = Object.freeze([
  {title: "Functional JavaScript"},
  {title: "Programming Elixir"}
]);

books.push({});
//Cannot add property 0

books.pop();
//Cannot delete property '0'
```

Add

Here is an example of adding a new value to an immutable array:

```
const newBook =
      Object.freeze({ title:"How JavaScript Works" });

//add with spread operator
const newBooks = [...books, newBook];

//add with concat()
const newBooks = books.concat([newBook]);
```

Remove

Below is an example of removing the value from position `index`:

```
const index = 0;
const newBooks = [...books.slice(0, index),
                  ...books.slice(index+1)];
```

`slice(start, end)` returns a portion of an array, between two specified indexes, as a new array. When the `end` index is omitted, all elements from the `start` position to the end of the array are selected. When the `start` index is also omitted, it starts from index 0 and makes a shallow clone of the array.

Edit

`map()` can be used to edit an element in an immutable array. The mapping function returns the new value for the element we want to update and returns the existing value for all the other elements.

```
const newBook = Object.freeze({title:"JavaScript Patterns"});
const editIndex = 0;

const newBooks = books.map(function(book, index){
    if(index === editIndex){
      return newBook;
    }

    return book;
  });
```

Immutable library

Immutable.js provides immutable data structures like `List` and `Map`. These data structures are highly optimized.

List

Let's work with the `List` data structure.

```
import { List } from "immutable";

const books = List([
  { title: "JavaScript Allongé" },
```

```
  { title: "You Don't Know JS" }
]);
```

Add

> push(value) returns a new List with the new value added.

```
const aNewBook = { title: "Mastering Immutable.js" };

const newBooks = books.push(aNewBook);

console.log(Array.from(books));
//[{title: "JavaScript Allongé"},
// {title: "You Don't Know JS"}]

console.log(Array.from(newBooks));
//[{title: "JavaScript Allongé"},
// {title: "You Don't Know JS"},
// {title: "Mastering Immutable.js"}]
```

Edit

> set(index, value) returns a new List having the new value
> at position index.

```
const aNewBook = { title: "Mastering Immutable.js" };

const newBooks = books.set(0, aNewBook);

console.log(Array.from(newBooks));
//[{title: "Mastering Immutable.js"},
// {title: "You Don't Know JS"}];
```

Remove

> remove(index) returns a new List with the value at the
> index position removed.

```
const newBooks = books.remove(0);

console.log(Array.from(newBooks));
//[{title: "You Don't Know JS"}];
```

Map

Next, let's loot at Map:

```
import { Map } from "immutable";

const book = Map({
  title: "The Square and the Tower",
  author: "Niall Ferguson"
});
```

Add

> set(key, value) returns a new Map containing the new key-value pair. If the key already exists, the value will be replaced. It can be used for both adding or editing a property.

```
const description = "Networks and Hierarchies";
const bookWithDesc = book.set("description", description);

console.log(bookWithDesc.toObject());
//{title:"The Square and the Tower",
// author:"Niall Ferguson",
// description:"Networks and Hierarchies"}
```

Edit

```
const title = "Civilization";
const newBook = book.set("title", title);

console.log(book.toObject());
//{title: "The Square and the Tower",
// author: "Niall Ferguson"}

console.log(newBook.toObject());
//{title: "Civilization",
// author: "Niall Ferguson"}
```

Remove

> remove(key) returns a new Map without the specified key.

```
const newBook = book.remove("author");
```

```
console.log(newBook.toObject());
//{title: "The Square and the Tower"}
```

I like the public interface of the `List` data structure but I find working with `Map` not so nice as working with an object literal. When working with `Map`, we need to access all properties as strings. There is no dot notation, so we need to get conformable with the string syntax.

The immutable `List` data structure can be converted to a native array using `Array.from()`, spread operator or the `toArray()` method. The `Map` data structure can be converted to an object literal with the `toObject()` method. These conversions can be slow for big arrays/objects.

For both processing and memory we should take in consideration immutable data structure provided by libraries like Immutable.js.

Transfer objects

Transfer objects are plain objects containing only data that move around the application from one function to another.

To avoid any unexpected changes they should be immutable.

Input values

Unexpected changes can create bugs hard to find and understand. That will mean more time to investigate problems, so immutability saves troubleshooting and debugging time.

All input values should be treated as immutable values regardless if they are or not. This way we avoid creating unexpected changes somewhere else in the application.

Change detection

Immutability offers efficiency at detecting change in an object. To detect if an object has changed, we just need to compare the previous reference with the current one. There is no need to check the values of all properties.

Final thoughts

Immutability makes code easier to read. When values cannot change, code is much easier to reason about.

Immutability avoids a set of hard to detect bugs.

There are two ways for working with immutable values in JavaScript. One is to freeze all objects and arrays at creation and then use the spread operator or the pure array methods to create new arrays. The other option is to use a library like Immutable.js that offers immutable data structures.

Immutability is not about variables that cannot change, but about values that cannot change.

Chapter 8: Partial application and currying

Partial application and currying are techniques for transforming functions into other functions with fewer arguments. They have a similar purpose, but they work in different ways. Let's see how.

Partial application

Partial application is the process of fixing a number of arguments to a function by producing another function with fewer arguments. The returned function is a partially applied function.

Fixing or binding the first arguments to a function creates a new function that takes the remaining arguments. Consider function f(x, y, z):

```
function f(x, y, z){
  console.log(x);
  console.log(y);
  console.log(z);
}

const f1 = partial(f, 1);
const f2 = partial(f, 1, 2);
const f3 = partial(f, 1, 2, 3);

f1(10, 100);
//1
//10
//1000
```

```
f2(4);
//1
//2
//4

f3();
//1
//2
//3
```

- Fixing one argument to function **f** creates a new function with two arguments.
- Fixing two arguments to the function creates a function with one argument.
- Fixing all three arguments creates a function with no arguments.

Imagine you have a function and you want to create another one accepting fewer arguments. First of all, why would you want that? One reason may be that you want to create a specialized function from a generic one. Another reason may be that you actually need a function that takes less arguments and can be use with functions like `filter()` or `map()`.

Next, we will look at utilities for doing partial application.

bind()

The `bind()` method can do partial application, however the value given to `this` requires attention. Take a look at the next example:

```
function log(level, message){
  console.log(level + " : "+message);
}

const logInfo = log.bind(null, "Info");
logInfo("A message");
//Info : A message
```

Notice how `logInfo()` function is created. It requires only one argument the `message`. `logInfo()` is a partially applied function.

partial()

To better understand how partial application works, let's create our own `partial()` function decorator.

`partial()` creates a version of the function that takes fewer arguments than the original function.

```
function partial(fn, ...leftArgs) {
  return function(...rightArgs) {
    return fn(...leftArgs, ...rightArgs);
  }
}

function log(level, message){
  console.log(level + " : "+message);
}

const logInfo = partial(log, "Info");
logInfo("A message");
//Info : A message
```

The `partial()` function can be found in libraries like lodash.js or underscore.js.

Partial application with filter

Partial application comes in handy when the new function is used as a callback and can take fewer arguments. Consider the next example:

```
function isTodoOfType(type, todo){
  return todo.type === type;
}

function getTodos(todos, type){
  return todos.filter(todo => isTodoOfType(type, todo));
}

const todos = [
 {id: 1, type: "NC", title: "create"},
 {id: 2, type: "RE", title: "review"}
];
```

```
const filteredTodos = getTodos(todos, "NC");
//[{id:1, type:"NC", title:"create"}];
```

The anonymous predicate for `filter()` takes one argument, the current `todo`, and uses it to call `isTodoOfType()`.

Another option is to use partial application and create a new function with the `type` already set:

```
const isOfType = partial(isTodoOfType, type);
```

Then we can use the new predicate function as a callback for the `filter()` method. Here is the code:

```
function getTodos(type){
  const isOfType = partial(isTodoOfType, type);
  return todos.filter(isOfType, type);
}
```

Arguments order

The arguments order is important.

The `partial()` utility fixes arguments from left to right. The following code will not work properly:

```
function isTodoOfType(todo, type){
  return todo.type === type;
}
```

```
function getTodos(type){
  return todos.filter(partial(isTodoOfType, type));
}
```

Notice the order of arguments in the `isTodoOfType(todo, type)` function. `partial(isTodoOfType, type)` sets the first argument `todo` with a value for `type`, which is wrong.

Partial application with map

Let's take the case of a shopping list containing the `productId` and `quantity` on each line item. Suppose we want to display all product details on each line. We can use the `map()` method to transform the shopping list into a new list with all product details. I would like to use the `toProductView(products, line)` function, but `map()` sends only one argument, the current line item. Here, partial application is useful for creating a new function with the **products** argument already set.

```
import partial from "lodash/partial";

const shoppingList = [
  {
    productId: 1,
    quantity: 2
  },
  {
    productId: 2,
    quantity: 1
  }
];

const products = {
  1 : { id: 1, name: "mango"},
  2 : { id: 2, name: "apple"}
}

function toProductView(products, line){
  const product = products[line.productId];
  return {
    ...line,
    ...product
  }
}

const newList = shoppingList
  .map(partial(toProductView, products));

console.log(newList);
//[
//{id: 1, name: "mango", quantity: 2},
//{id: 2, name: "apple", quantity: 1}
//]
```

Partial application with event handlers

Partial application provides a nice way to pass arguments to event handlers. Check the next example in React:

```
import partial from "lodash/partial";

function TodoItem({ todo, onRemoveClick }) {
  return (
    <li>
      <div>{todo.title}</div>
      <button onClick={partial(onRemoveClick, todo)}>
        Delete
      </button>
    </li>
  );
}
```

Currying

> Currying transforms a function that takes multiple arguments into a sequence of functions where each takes one argument.

Consider for example the f(x,y,z) function with three arguments. Here is how we can write the curried version:

```
function f(x){
  return function(y){
    return function(z){
      console.log(x);
      console.log(y);
      console.log(z);
    }
  }
}

f(1)(2)(3);
//1
//2
//3
```

A curried function is a function that takes multiple arguments one at a time and returns a sequence of unary functions until all arguments have been provided.

Applying all arguments to the function executes the function.

```
f(1); // returns a function
f(1)(2); //returns a function
f(1)(2)(3); //executes f and returns the result
```

Currying with filter

Let's take the previous situation, where isTodoOfType() needs two arguments and we want to use it with filter() that provides only one of them, the todo.

The isTodoOfType can be created as a curried function. It takes the type and returns a predicate function that takes the todo and returns a boolean. See the code below:

```
function isTodoOfType(type){
  return function(todo){
    return todo.type === type;
  }
};

function getTodos(type){
 return todos.filter(isTodoOfType(type));
}

const todos = [
 {id: 1, type: "NC", title: "create"},
 {id: 2, type: "RE", title: "review"}
];

const filteredTodos = getTodos("NC");
//[{id:1, type:"NC", title:"create"}];
```

Currying with map

In the shopping list example, we can rewrite the toProductView() function, that needs two arguments, as a curried function. Consider the next code:

```
function toProductView(products){
```

```
  return function(line){
    const product = products[line.productId];
    return {
      ...line,
      ...product
    }
  }
}

const newList = shoppingList.map(toProductView(products));
```

curry()

In functional languages like Haskell, functions are curried by default. Calling the function with fewer arguments results in a new function taking the remaining arguments. Calling the function with all arguments executes the function.

In JavaScript currying can be enabled with an utility function like curry().

curry() offers a more flexible apply system than a truly curried function. It can apply multiple arguments at once, not just one. When applying all arguments the function is executed.

```
import { curry } from 'lodash';

const f = curry(function(x, y, z){
  console.log(x);
  console.log(y);
  console.log(z);
});

f(1, 2, 3);
f(1, 2)(3);
f(1)(2)(3);
//1
//2
//3
```

Here is an implementation of the curry() function:

```
function curry(f, leftArgs = []){
  return function(...args){
```

```
    const allArgs = [...leftArgs, ...args];
    if (allArgs.length >= f.length) {
      return f(...allArgs);
    } else{
      return curry(f, allArgs);
    }
  }
}
```

This implementation of the **curry()** function doesn't work correctly with functions having a rest parameter or default values.

The function **length** property gets the number of parameters the function is expecting. However, the rest parameter does not count into the function length property, neither default values.

```
function f1 (a, b) { }
function f2 (a, ...b) { }
function f3 (a, b=0) { }


f1.length; //2
f2.length; //1
f3.length; //1
```

A solution would be to take a parameter, specifying the number of parameters.

```
function curry(f, length, leftArgs = []){
  let noArguments = f.length;
  if(length) {
    noArguments = length;
  }

  return function(...args){
    const allArgs = [...leftArgs, ...args];
    if (allArgs.length >= noArguments){
      return f(...allArgs);
    } else{
      return curry(f, length, allArgs);
    }
  }
}
```

```
function f(a, b=0) {
  console.log(a);
  console.log(b);
}

const fn = curry(f, 2);
fn(1)(2);
//1
//2
```

The curry() function can be found in lodash.js or ramda.js.

Arity

The arity of a function represents the numbers of arguments it takes.

- A unary function is a function that takes one argument.
- A binary function takes two arguments.
- A ternary function takes three arguments.
- An n-ary function takes n arguments.
- A nullary function takes no arguments.

Partial application and currying decrease the arity of a function.

Currying transforms a n-ary function into n unary functions.

Full Application

Applying fewer than the total number of arguments to a function is a partial application.

Applying all arguments to a function is a full application.

Consider the following full applications of the f(x, y, z) function:

```
function f(x, y, z){
  console.log(x);
  console.log(y);
  console.log(z);
}

f(1,2,3);
f.apply(null, [1,2,3]);
f.call(null, 1,2,3);
```

Applying all arguments to a curried function is a full application and executes the function.

```
const fn = curry(f);
fn(1)(2)(3);
```

The partial utility functions are an exception. Applying all arguments to a function with **partial()** creates a nullary function with all arguments fixed. The original function is not executed immediately when the arguments are applied. This new function can be used as a callback.

```
const fn = partial(f,1,2,3);
setTimeout(fn, 1000);
//1
//2
//3
```

Thunk

A thunk is a function that delays the invocation of another function. The thunk function calls the original function with all arguments.

```
function sum(x, y, z){
  const total = x + y + z;
  console.log(total);
  return total;
}

function sumThunk() {
  return sum(1, 2, 3);
}

sumThunk();
//6
```

We can use function decorators to create thunks.

thunk(fn, args) takes a function and all the arguments and creates a new function that executes the original function with all arguments.

```
function thunk(fn, ...args){
  return function(){
    return fn(...args);
  }
```

```
}
```

```
const sumFirst3 = thunk(sum, 1, 2, 3);
setTimeout(sumFirst3, 3000);
//6 after 3s
```

thunkify(fn) takes a function fn and returns a new function that asks for arguments and returns a third function that, when called, invokes fn with the all arguments.

```
function thunkify(fn) {
  return function(...args) {
    return function() {
      return fn(...args);
    }
  }
}
```

```
const sumFirst3 = thunkify(sum)(1, 2, 3);
setTimeout(sumFirst3, 3000);
//6 after 3s
```

I think is better to use **partial()** only with fewer arguments than the total number of arguments, and use **thunk()** to create a nullary function that calls the original function with all arguments.

```
function f(x, y, z){
  console.log(x);
  console.log(y);
  console.log(z);
}
```

```
const fThunk = thunk(f, 1, 2, 3);
$("#btn").click(fThunk);
```

Final thoughts

Partial application transforms a function with multiple arguments in a function with fewer arguments.

Currying transforms a function with multiple arguments in a sequence of functions each taking one argument.

Chapter 9: Function composition

Function composition is a technique of passing the output of a function as the input for another function.

Suppose we have two function `f()` and `g()` taking one argument.

```
const y = g(x);
const z = f(y);
```

Composing them means:

```
const z = f(g(x));
```

compose()

In order to compose multiple functions we can create the `compose()` utility function.

```
f(g(x)) === compose(f,g)(x);
```

Here is an implementation for `compose()`:

```
function compose(...functions){
  return function(x){
    return functions.reduceRight((value,f) => f(value), x);
  }
}

function f(y){
  return y * y;
}
```

```
function g(x){
  return x + x;
}

f(g(2)) === compose(f,g)(2);
```

`compose()` works with unary functions.

Composing with decorators

Consider the following code selecting the `title` from a collection of books:

```
import prop from "lodash/property";

const books = [
  {id:1, title: "JavaScript The Good Parts", type: "T"},
  {id:2, title: "Civilization", type: "H"},
  {id:3, title: "Javascript Allongé", type: "T"}
];

const titles = books.map(prop("title"));
//["JavaScript The Good Parts",
// "Civilization",
// "Javascript Allongé"]
```

In this case, we use function composition. The `map()` function takes as input the return value from the `prop()` function.

Below is another example of function composition using `matchesProperty()` to find a book by id:

```
import matchesProperty from "lodash/matchesProperty";

const book = books.find(matchesProperty("id", 1));
//{id: 1, title: "JavaScript The Good Parts", type: "T"}
```

Function `find()` takes as input the return value from `matchesProperty()` decorator.

When composing functions this way the first function can have multiple arguments.

pipe()

pipe() creates a pipeline of functions, where the output of one function is the input for the next one.

Consider the next code:

```
function filterBooks(todos){
  return todos.filter(isTechnology);
}

function isTechnology(todo){
  return todo.type === "T";
}

function creatItemHtml(todo){
  return `<div>${todo.title}</div>`;
}

function createListHtml(todos){
  const htmlArr = todos.map(creatItemHtml);
  return htmlArr.join("");
}

function renderHtml(html){
  $("#books").html(html);
}

const books = [
  { id:1, title: "JavaScript The Good Parts", type: "T" },
  { id:2, title: "Civilization", type: "H" },
  { id:3, title: "Javascript Allongé", type: "T" }
];

const filteredBooks = filterBooks(books);
const html = createListHtml(filteredBooks);
renderHtml(html);
```

The books processing can be rewritten with the pipe() utility function:

```
import pipe from "lodash/flow";

pipe(
```

```
  filterBooks,
  createListHtml,
  renderHtml
)(books);
```

A utility function like `logData()` can be used to log data between transformations:

```
import pipe from "lodash/flow";

function logData(data){
  console.log(data)
  return data;
}

pipe(
  filterBooks,
  logData,
  createListHtml,
  logData,
  renderHtml
)(books);
```

Here is an implementation for the `pipe()` function:

```
function pipe(...functions){
  return function(x){
    return functions.reduce((value, f) => f(value), x);
  }
}
```

`pipe()` works with functions taking one argument.

Composing with promise chaining

When we use promise chaining we use function composition. The result of one function is passed as input for the next function. Look at the next example:

```
function fetchBooks() {
  return new Promise(function(resolve, reject) {
    resolve(books);
  });
}
```

```
function handleError(error) {
  console.error(error);
}

fetchBooks()
  .then(filterBooks)
  .then(createListHtml)
  .then(renderHtml)
  .catch(handleError);
```

Final thoughts

Function composition is the process of applying one function to the result of another. With function composition we eliminate the intermediary variables.

Pipelines make data transformations more expressive.

Chapter 10: Intention revealing names

Choosing good names takes time but saves more than it takes. So take care with your names and change them when you find better ones. Everyone who reads your code, including you, will be happier if you do.

The name of a variable, function ... should answer all the big questions. It should tell you why it exists, what it does, and how it is used. If a name requires a comment, then the name does not reveal its intent.— Tim Ottinger in Clean Code

The function name turns out to have a very important role in readability as we can easily read and understand meaningful words. The function name is our tool for expressing the intention on a piece of code.

Refactoring anonymous functions

Functions can be created with or without a name. The arrow syntax usually creates anonymous functions. Consider the following code written with anonymous arrow functions:

```
const books = [
  {title:"How JavaScript works",type:"T"},
  {title:"Square and tower",type:"H"},
  {title:"Functional-Light JavaScript",type:"T"}
];

const newBooks = books
  .filter(book => book.type === "T")
  .sort((book1, book2) => {
```

```
    if(book1.title < book2.title) return -1;
    if(book1.title > book2.title) return 1;
    return 0;
 });
```

```
//[{title:"Functional-Light JavaScript",type:"T"},
// {title:"How JavaScript works",type:"T"}];
```

Now check out the same logic refactored to pure functions with intention revealing names:

```
function isTechnology(book){
    return book.type === "T";
}
```

```
function ascByTitle(book1, book2){
    if(book1.title<book2.title) return -1;
    if(book1.title>book2.title) return 1;
    return 0;
}
```

```
const newBooks = books
                .filter(isTechnology)
                .sort(ascByTitle);
```

With good function names we can read the code faster. We can read the function name and understand its purpose. There is no need to analyze its code.

Let's look at an event handler written with an anonymous function.

```
$("#first").click(() => {
    const list = getItemsFromList();
    const filteredList = list.slice(0,1);
    renderList(filteredList);
});
```

Below is the code after refactoring to a function with a clear name:

```
$("#first").click(renderFirstItem);
```

```
function renderFirstItem(){
    const list = getItemsFromList();
    const filteredList = list.slice(0,1);
```

```
  renderList(filteredList);
}
```

I suggest to use names that express the function purse and add
value to existing code. For example, names like onClick() or
myCustomClickEvent() express where the function is used not what it
does. The same function can very well handle other events or be called in
other places.

Named function expressions

Next, we will look at how to improve readability with named function
expressions.

I will exaggerate the situation and use three anonymous IIFEs:

```
(() => {
    /*code*/
    (() => {
        /*code*/
        (() => {
            /*code*/
        })();
    })();
})();
```

Anonymous functions appear as (anonymous) in the CallStack.

▼ Call Stack	
➦ (anonymous)	(index):74
(anonymous)	(index):75
(anonymous)	(index):76

Let's rewrite the code with named function expressions:

```
(function createTodoModule(){
  /*code*/
  (function getAllTodos(){
    /*code*/
    (function renderTodo(){
      /*code*/
    })();
  })();
```

```
})();
```

This time, the Call Stack is easier to understand.

▼ Call Stack	
◆ renderTodo	(index):85
getAllTodos	(index):86
createTodoModule	(index):87

`createTodoModule()`, `getAllTodos()` and `renderTodo()` are named function expressions.

Names with arrow functions

I think that names can improve readability in cases with little logic. Let's take the example of computing a sum over an array.

```
//using anonymous function
const total = numbers.reduce((a, b) => a + b, 0);
```

```
//using named function
function sum(a, b) { return a + b; }
const total = numbers.reduce(sum, 0);
```

The `sum()` function can be written with the arrow syntax. In this case, the arrow function infers the name of the variable.

```
const sum = (a, b) => a + b;
const total = numbers.reduce(sum, 0);
```

Simple code

There are situation when the code is so small that creating a named function adds no value. In that case, we can stay with the anonymous function until the code becomes more complex. Consider the next code:

```
const books = [
  {title:"How JavaScript works",type:"T"},
  {title:"Square and tower",type:"H"},
  {title:"Functional-Light JavaScript",type:"T"}
];
```

```
const titles = books.map(book => book.title);
```

```
//["How JavaScript works", "Square and tower",
// "Functional-Light JavaScript"]
```

Another option is to use a generic utility function like `prop()`:

```
import prop from "lodash/property";

const titles = books.map(prop("title"));
```

Arrow function vs `function`

Less code doesn't necessary mean more readable. The next example shows two ways for defining the `prop()` function. I prefer the one using the `function` keyword as I think it is clearer what the function does.

`prop()` takes the name of a property and returns a function that asks for an object an returns the property of that object.

```
//with arrow function
const prop = key => obj => obj[key];

//with function keyword
function prop(key){
   return function(obj){
      return obj[key];
   }
}
```

Final thoughts

Intention revealing function names improve readability and offer a better debugging experience.

I suggest to refactor to a named function whenever the name adds value to the existing code.

Chapter 11: Making code easier to read

I believe very deeply that the vastly more important role of code is as a means of communication with other human beings.

It's widely estimated that developers spend 70% of code maintenance time on reading to understand it.— Kyle Simpson, author of Functional-Light JavaScript

Developers have an easier time understanding small pieces of code with intention revealing names. Understanding is easier if functions are pure.

Let's look at how we can improve code readability with functional programming techniques.

Refactoring with filter and map

I will take the case of a collection of to-dos:

```
const todos = [
  {
    id : 1,
    type : "NC",
    desc : "task1",
    user : { id: 1, name: "user1"},
    completed : false
  },
  {
    id : 2,
    type : "RE",
    desc : "task2",
```

```
      user : { id: 2, name: "user2"},
      completed : false
   }
];
```

Below is the imperative code filtering the to-dos and creating new objects having the `userName` property.

```
let filteredTodos = [];
for(let i=0; i<todos.length; i++){
  let todo = todos[i];
  if (todo.type === "RE" && !todo.completed) {
    filteredTodos.push({...todo,userName: todo.user.name});
  }
}
```

```
console.log(filteredTodos);
//[{
// completed: false,
// desc: "task2",
// id: 2,
// type: "RE",
// user: {id: 2, name: "user2"},
// userName: "user2"
//}]
```

Refactoring to a functional style makes use of the `filter()` and `map()` functions.

```
const filteredTodos = todos
 .filter(todo => (todo.type === "RE" && !todo.completed))
 .map(todo => ({ ...todo, userName: todo.user.name }));
```

> Chaining is a technique used to simplify code where multiple methods are applied to an object one after another.

`map()` and `filter()` are chained.

We can improve the code further by extracting out the anonymous callbacks and give them intention revealing names. See the code below:

```
function isPriorityTodo(todo){
   return todo.type === "RE" && !todo.completed;
}
```

```
function toTodoView(todo) {
    return { ...todo, userName: todo.user.name };
}

const filteredTodos = todos
 .filter(todo => isPriorityTodo(todo))
 .map(todo => toTodoView(todo));
```

isPriorityTodo() and toTodoView() are pure functions with intention revealing names.

Point-free style

> Point-free is a technique that improves readability by elimi-
> nating the unnecessary arguments.

Consider the previous code:

```
const filteredTodos = todos
 .filter(todo => isPriorityTodo(todo))
 .map(todo => toTodoView(todo));
```

Here is the code after eliminating the unnecessary arguments:

```
const filteredTodos = todos
  .filter(isPriorityTodo)
  .map(toTodoView);
```

The point-free style can improve readability in specific places.

There is no `function` keyword, no arrow syntax in a point-free style. That means we use another function to create the function we need. All we see in a point-free style are function names.

Refactoring with reduce

Let's take the case of a shopping list:

```
const shoppingList = [
    {name: "orange", quantity: 2, price: 10, type: "FRT"},
    {name: "lemon", quantity: 1, price: 15, type: "FRT"},
    {name: "fish", quantity: 0.5, price: 30, type: "MET"}
];
```

Below is the imperative code computing the total price and the price for fruits:

```
let totalPrice = 0, fruitsPrice = 0;
for(let i=0; i<shoppingList.length; i++){
    let line = shoppingList[i];
    totalPrice += line.quantity * line.price;
    if (line.type === "FRT") {
        fruitsPrice += line.quantity * line.price;
    }
}


console.log(totalPrice);
//50
console.log(fruitsPrice);
//35
```

Taking the functional approach in this case will require the use of **reduce()** to compute the total price.

> **reduce()** reduces a list of values to one value

As we did before, we refactor the code using pure functions with intention revealing names, pure array methods and a point-free style:

```
function addPrice(totalPrice, line){
    return totalPrice + (line.quantity * line.price);
}

function areFruits(line){
    return line.type === "FRT";
}

let totalPrice = shoppingList.reduce(addPrice, 0);
let fruitsPrice = shoppingList
                .filter(areFruits)
                .reduce(addPrice, 0);
```

Decomposition

Our natural way of dealing with a problem is to break it into smaller pieces and then put everything back together.

Our aim should be to create small pure functions with intention revealing names and then compose them back together.

Naming these small functions requires time, but if it is done well, it will make the code easier to read.

There will be two kinds of functions:

- Functions doing one task
- Functions coordinating a lot of tasks. Here we can use a point-free style to make code easier to read.

Final thoughts

Working with collections in a functional style breaks the data transformations in steps like filter, map, reduce or sort. At the same time, it requires to define small pure functions to support those transformations.

The point-free style improves the code clarity and readability.

Functional programming together with the practice of giving intention revealing names greatly improves code readability.

Chapter 12: Asynchronous programming

In a sense, there are two kind of functions: synchronous and asynchronous.

A synchronous function returns only after the operation is finished.

An asynchronous function starts the operation and returns immediately. The operation may finish somewhere in the future.

In a console application, a command like `Console.ReadKey()` blocks the program until a character is pressed. This kind of approach may work for a console application where you cannot do anything else anyway, but it doesn't work for a web application.

Synchronous code is easy to reason about, but there are situations where we need to do things without blocking the interface. Looking from this perspective:

Synchronous code is blocking.

Asynchronous code is not blocking.

We need a way to listen for user interactions or to get data from Web APIs without blocking the interface. This is the role of the asynchronous programming model.

Blocking vs not blocking

The sequential model blocks the program for input/output or for any long running process. The asynchronous model doesn't block. Consider the next code:

```
function block(duration){
  const starTime = Date.now();
  while (Date.now() < starTime + duration) {}
}

function logMessage(){
  console.log("process ended");
}

block(5000);
logMessage();
```

This is an example of a blocking code. It blocks everything for 5s and then executes the `logMessage()` function. When the application is blocked, it is unresponsive.

Let's see how to display a message, after an interval, without blocking.

```
function logMessage(){
  console.log("process ended");
}

function delay(duration, callback){
  setTimeout(callback, duration);
}

delay(5000, logMessage);
```

This time the application is not blocked. After 5s the message is displayed.

An asynchronous function returns immediately because it just starts the work to be done. It doesn't wait for it to finish.

The most common asynchronous tasks are: user events, networks calls, timing events.

Callbacks

Callbacks offer a simple way to run code when asynchronous operations are completed.

> A callback is a function passed as an argument to another function.

The most common scenarios where callbacks are used for asynchronous tasks are events.

DOM events

User interactions may result in many events like `click`, `focus`, `blur`, `keypress`. Listening for this events doesn't block the interface.

Look at the next examples using callbacks to handle DOM events with jQuery:

```
function doSomething(){ }

$("#btn").on("click", doSomething);
$("#input").on("keypress", doSomething);
```

Here is an another example with React:

```
import React from "react";

function TodoItem({ todo, onRemoveClick }) {
  return (
    <div>
      <div>{todo.title}</div>
      <div>
      <button onClick={onRemoveClick}>
        Delete
      </button>
      </div>
    </div>
  );
}
```

Timing events

There are two functions for executing code at specified time intervals.

`setTimeout`: executes a callback once after an interval. It can be cancelled with `clearTimeout()`.

`setInterval`: executes a callback at a specific interval. It runs until the `clearInterval` function is called.

```
setInterval(doSomething, 5000);
```

Nested callbacks

Callback are great for simple tasks like event handling, but they are hard to combine. Consider `fetchUsers()`, `fetchPosts()`, `fetchComments()` as being able to do network calls and accept a callback to execute when the operation is completed.

```
fetchUsers(function(users) {
  fetchPosts(function(dictionaries) {
    fetchComments(function(todos) {
      console.log(users);
      console.log(dictionaries);
      console.log(todos);
    });
  });
});
```

What about starting all network calls at the same time and then do something? It is possible with callbacks, but it is harder and can make code more complicated than necessary.

Promises

Promises offer a better option for composing asynchronous tasks.

> A promise is an object that represents a possible future result of an asynchronous operation.

Promises can be given to some other parts of the code before knowing the result.

Network calls

Promises are commonly used to handle network calls. The application is not blocked while waiting for the Web API response. Even more, the network calls can run in parallel.

Network calls can be done with the `fetch()` function. The `fetch()` function returns a promise.

Composing promises

Let's look at how to compose promises:

```
function fetchUsers() {
```

```
  return fetch("/users");
}

function fetchPosts() {
  return fetch("/posts");
}

function fetchComments() {
  return fetch("/comments");
}

function doSomething() { }

function handleError(error) {
  console.error(error);
}

fetchUsers()
  .then(fetchPosts)
  .then(fetchComments)
  .then(doSomething)
  .catch(handleError);
```

Promises support a chaining system that allows to pass data through a set of functions. Promises use callbacks.

Note the execution flow in the previous example:

- `fetchPosts` executes after `fetchUsers` gets the result. The application is not blocked while waiting for its result.
- `fetchComments` executes after `fetchPosts` gets the result.

The result of `fetchUsers` is passed as input to `fetchPosts`. The result of `fetchUsers` is passed as input to `fetchComments` and so on.

The data flow is : `fetchUsers` → `fetchPosts` → `fetchComments` → `doSomething`

If there is an error at any step, the chain control jumps to the closest rejection handler down the chain.

`Promise.all()` returns a new promise that resolves when all promises have resolved, or rejects when one of the promises rejects.

`Promise.race()` returns a new promise that resolves or rejects when one promise resolves or rejects.

```
const allPromises = [ fetchUsers(),
                      fetchPosts(),
                      fetchComments() ];

Promise.all(allPromises)
  .then(doSomething)
  .catch(handleError);
```

async/await

`async/await` allows to write asynchronous code that looks like synchronous code. `async/await` is a syntactical sugar for using promises.

The syntax requires to mark functions with the `async` keyword.

```
//async with function declaration
async function doAsynchronousTask() {}

//async with arrow function
const doAsynchronousTask = async ()=>{ };
```

Let's see how to use other asynchronous tasks inside a function. Check the next example:

```
(async function startApplication(){
  const users = await fetchUsers();
  const posts = await fetchPosts();
  const comments = await fetchComments();
  console.log(users);
  console.log(posts);
  console.log(comments);
})();
```

The `await` operator is used to wait for a promise.

The code after `await fetchUsers()` executes when `fetchUsers` gets the result. The code after `await fetchPosts()` executes when `fetchPosts` gets the result. In a way, it can be imagined like:

```
fetchUsers().then((users) => {
  fetchPosts().then((posts) => {
```

```
    fetchComments().then((comments)=>{
      console.log(users);
      console.log(posts);
      console.log(comments);
    });
  });
});
```

try/catch is used to handle errors.

```
function handleError(error) {
    console.error(error);
}

(async function startApplication() {
  try {
    const users = await fetchUsers();
    const posts = await fetchPosts();
    const comments = await fetchComments();
  } catch(error) {
    handleError(error);
  }
})();
```

The previous code can be imagined as:

```
fetchUsers()
 .then((users) => {
   fetchPosts().then((posts) => {
     fetchComments().then((comments)=>{
     });
   });
 })
 .catch(handleError);
```

When we want to execute all network calls in parallel, we can use `await` with `Promise.all()`:

```
(async function startApplication(){
  const allPromises = [ fetchUsers(),
                        fetchPosts(),
                        fetchComments() ];
  const [todos, users, albums] =
```

```
    await Promise.all(allPromises);
  console.log(todos);
  console.log(users);
  console.log(albums);
})();
```

I don't think that making asynchronous code look like synchronous code is necessarily a good idea. It may lead to trouble understanding which code is executed asynchronously and which is executed synchronously. I think that promises are clearer at showing which part of the code deals with asynchronous tasks.

The Event Loop

The JavaScript engine runs in a single thread. At one moment, a single line of code is executed.

JavaScript has a simpler asynchronous programming model without threads, race conditions, locks or deadlocks.

The engine uses an event loop. Callback functions are added to the event loop when an event occurs and there is an event listener attached to it. The event loop uses a queue, so callbacks are processed in the order they are added.

Functions in the event loop must finish fast. If they don't the application becomes unresponsive and after some minutes the browser displays the "script is taking too long to run" dialog.

DOM events, timing events, network requests, all add callbacks to the event loop.

The next code doesn't finish fast and blocks the application:

```
for(let i=0; i<10000000000; i++){}
```

Web Workers

Web workers offer a way to run long running tasks. These tasks run in parallel and don't affect the main thread. When a long running task finishes, the result must be communicated back to the main thread.

There is no shared memory between the main thread and web workers.

In the next example, the main thread creates a web worker and sends it a message to start the long running process. It then listens for the result and after terminates the worker.

```
const worker = new Worker("worker.js");

//send message to worker
worker.postMessage("start");

//receive message from worker
worker.onmessage = function(e) {
  console.log(e.data);
  worker.terminate();
};
```

The worker listens for messages from the main thread. When it gets the "start" message, it begins the long running computation. After the computation finishes, the result is sent to the main thread with postMessage().

```
function computeValue() {
  for (let i = 0; i < 10000000000; i++) {}
  return 10000000000;
}

//receive message from main thread
onmessage = function(e) {
  const action = e.data;
  if (action === "start") {
    const result = computeValue();

    //send message to main thread
    postMessage(result);
  }
};
```

Final thoughts

Callbacks are the fundamental unit of asynchronous programming.

Promises are objects that represent future results. Promises offer a better way for composing asynchronous tasks.

`async/await` allows to write asynchronous code that looks like synchronous code.

JavaScript offers a simpler asynchronous programming model without threads, race conditions, locks or deadlocks.

Web workers can run long running tasks.

Chapter 13: Objects with prototypes

Objects are dynamic collections of properties with a "hidden" property to the object's prototype. The property has a key and a value.

Property key

The property key is a unique string.

There are two ways to access properties: dot notation and bracket notation. When the dot notation is used, the property key must be a valid identifier.

```
const obj = {
  message : "discover"
}
```

```
obj.message; //"discover"
```

Accessing a property that doesn't exist will not throw an error, but will return **undefined** .

```
obj.otherProperty; //undefined
```

When the bracket notation is used, the property key does not have to be a valid identifier, it can have any value.

```
const french = {};
french["Thank you"] = "Merci";
```

```
french["Thank you"]; //"Merci"
```

When a value, that is not a string, is used as the property key, it is converted to a string, via the `toString()` method when available.

```
const obj = {};

//Number as key
obj[1] = "Number 1";
obj[1] === obj['1']; //true

//Object as key
const number1 = {
  toString : function() {return '1';}
}
obj[number1] === obj['1']; //true
```

In the previous example, the object `number1` is used as the property key. It is then converted to a string and the result of the conversion, `'1'`, is used as the property key.

Property value

The property value can be a primitive, an object or a function.

Object as value

Objects can be nested inside other objects. See the next example:

```
const book = {
  title : "How JavaScript Works",
  author : {
    firstName : "Douglas",
    lastName : "Crockford"
  }
}

book.author.firstName; //"Douglas"
```

This way, we can create a namespace:

```
const app = {};

app.authorGateway = {
  getAuthors : function() {}
```

```
};

app.bookGateway = {
  getBooks : function() {}
};
```

Function as value

When a function is used as a value for a property, it usually becomes a method. Inside methods, the **this** keyword is used to refer the current object. However, **this** can have many values depending on how the function is invoked.

Prototypes

Objects have a "hidden" link **__proto__** to the prototype object, from which they inherit properties.

For example, objects created with an object literal have a link to the **Object.prototype** :

```
const obj = {};
obj.__proto__ === Object.prototype; //true
```

Objects inherit from objects.

The prototypal inheritance has the benefit of memory conservation. The prototype is created once and used by all instances.

Prototype chain

The prototype object has a prototype of its own. When a property is accessed and the object does not contain it, the engine will look down the prototype objects until it either finds the requested property, or until it reaches **null**.

Read only

The prototype link is used only for reading values. When a change is made, it is made only on the current object not on its prototype, not even when a property with the same name exists on the prototype.

Built-in prototypes

Numbers inherit from `Number.prototype`, which inherits from `Object.prototype` .

```
let no = 1;
no.__proto__ === Number.prototype; //true
no.__proto__.__proto__ === Object.prototype; //true
```

Strings inherit from `String.prototype`. Booleans inherit from `Boolean.prototype`. Arrays inherit from `Array.prototype`. Functions inherit from `Function.prototype`.

All objects, functions and primitives, except `null` and **undefined**, inherit properties from `Object.prototype`. All of them have the `toString()` method, for example.

Map

We can think of an object as a map. The keys in the map are the names of the object's properties.

Accessing a key doesn't require to scan through all the properties. It is an $O(1)$ access time.

`Object.create(null)` creates an object with no prototype. Usually this is used to create a map.

```
const italian = Object.create(null);

italian["Yes"] = "Si";
italian["No"]  = "No";

italian["Yes"]; //"Si"
```

Object literal

Object literal offers a simple, elegant way for creating objects.

```
const timer = {
  secret: 0,
  start : function() {},
  stop : function() {},
}
```

However, this syntax has a few drawbacks. All properties are public, methods can be redefined, and we can't use the same methods on new instances.

```
timer.secret; //0
timer.start = function() {
  console.log("don't start");
}
timer.start(); //"don't start"
```

Object.create()

`Object.create(prototypeObject)` creates a new object, using the argument object as its prototype.

With `Object.create()` we can create a new `timer` object with `timerPrototype` as its prototype. This means that `start()` and `stop()` are available on the `timer` object. It also means that the `__proto__` property from `timer` points to the `timerPrototype` object.

```
const timerPrototype = {
  start : function() {},
  stop : function() {}
};

const timer = Object.create(timerPrototype);
timer.__proto__ === timerPrototype; //true
```

When the prototype is frozen, the objects that inherit from it won't be able to change the properties defined within. In this case, the `start()` and `stop()` methods can't be redefined.

```
const timerPrototype = Object.freeze({
  start : function() {},
  stop : function() {}
});

const timer = Object.create(timerPrototype);
timer.start = function() {
  console.log("don't start");
}
//Cannot assign to read only property 'start' of object
```

`Object.create(timerPrototype)` can be used to build more objects with the same prototype.

Function constructor

Initially, the language proposed the function constructor as a sugar syntax for building objects with a custom prototype. Take a look at the next example:

```
function Timer(){
  this.secret = 0;
}

Timer.prototype = {
  start : function() {},
  stop : function() {}
}

const timer = new Timer();
timer.start();
```

All functions defined with the `function` keyword can be used as function constructors. The function constructor is called with the `new` operator. The new object has the prototype set to FunctionConstructor.prototype.

```
const timer = new Timer();
timer.__proto__ === Timer.prototype;
```

To prevent method redefinition the prototype should be frozen.

```
Timer.prototype = Object.freeze({
  start : function() {},
  stop : function() {}
});
```

new

When `new Timer()` is executed it does similar steps as the `newTimer()` function:

```
function newTimer(){
  let newObj = Object.create(Timer.prototype);
  let returnObj = Timer.call(newObj, arguments);
  if(returnObj) return returnObj;
```

```
    return newObj;
}
```

A new object is created with `Timer.prototype` as its prototype. Then the `Timer` function runs and sets the fields on the new object.

Class

`class` offers a much better sugar syntax for building objects with a custom prototype. Check out the next example:

```
class Timer{
  constructor(){
    this.secret = 0;
  }

  start() {}
  stop() {}
}
```

Objects built with `class` have the prototype set to ClassName.prototype.

```
const timer = new Timer();
timer.__proto__ === Timer.prototype;
```

In order to avoid method redefinition we need to freeze the class' prototype.

```
Object.freeze(Timer.prototype);
```

No privacy

The prototype-based inheritance patterns have no privacy. All object's properties are public.

`Object.keys()` returns an array with all own property keys. It can be used to iterate over object's properties.

```
function logProperty(name){
  console.log(name); //property name
  console.log(obj[name]); //value
}

Object.keys(obj).forEach(logProperty);
```

Final thoughts

Objects are dynamic in nature and can be used as maps. All object's properties are public.

Objects inherit from other objects.

Constructor function and class are a sugar syntax for creating objects that inherit from a custom prototype object. They first define the custom prototype with all methods and then the **new** operator creates objects that inherit from that prototype.

Chapter 14: Objects with closures

> Closure - is a consequence of functions that can nest and functions that are first class values, and JavaScript has it, and is almost completely right in the way it implements them, and it's maybe the best feature ever put into a programming language.— Douglas Crockford

Closures can be created as functions with private state. More than that, we can create many closures sharing the same private state. This way, we can build objects as collections of closures. Closures encapsulate state.

Factory functions

Let's see how we can do that. We start form the Revealing Module pattern, give that function a name and use it to build new encapsulated objects. Here is an example of the `Counter` function that can create counter objects:

```
function Counter(){
    let state = 0;

    function increment(){
        state += 1;
        return state;
    }

    function decrement(){
        state -= 1;
        return state;
```

```
    }

    return Object.freeze({
        increment,
        decrement
    });
};

const counter = Counter();
counter.increment(); //1
counter.increment(); //2
counter.increment(); //3

const otherCounter = Counter();
otherCounter.increment(); //1
```

The Counter function is called factory function. Objects built this way have a series of benefits.

Encapsulation

Encapsulation means information hiding.

When using closures, only the methods exposed are public, everything else is encapsulated.

```
const counter = Counter();
counter.state; //undefined
```

The private data of the object can be modified only through its public methods.

Immutable public interface

The public interface of an object created using a factory function is immutable. Notice the use of Object.freeze() on the returned object containing the public methods.

```
const counter = Counter();
counter.increment = function() {
    console.log("don't increment");
}
//Cannot assign to read only property 'increment' of object
```

No this

There are no **this** changing context issues simply because when building objects with closures, **this** is not used at all.

Let's build a few other objects with closures and compare them with the ones built with prototypes.

Timer

The timer object is used to do asynchronous operations at a specific interval. In contrast with **setInterval** it waits for the previous operation to finish before making a new call. It implements the Recursive setTimeout pattern. Below the timer object is created both with prototypes and with closures

Timer with prototypes

```
class Timer {
  constructor(callback, interval){
    this.callback = callback;
    this.interval = interval;
    this.timerId = 0;
 }

  executeAndStartTimer(){
    this.callback().then(() => {
        this.timerId = setTimeout(this.executeAndStartTimer,
          this.interval);
    });
 }

  start(){
    if(this.timerId === 0){
      this.executeAndStartTimer();
    }
 }

  stop(){
    if(this.timerId !== 0){
      clearTimeout(this.timerId);
      this.timerId = 0;
    }
```

```
 }
}

function getTodos(){
  return fetch("/todos");
}

const timer = new Timer(getTodos,2000);
timer.start();
```

Timer with closures

```
function Timer(callback, interval){
  let timerId;

  function executeAndStartTimer(){
    callback().then(function makeNewCall(){
      timerId = setTimeout(executeAndStartTimer, interval);
    });
  }

  function stop(){
    if(timerId){
      clearTimeout(timerId);
      timerId = 0;
    }
  }

  function start(){
    if(!timerId){
      executeAndStartTimer();
    }
  }

  return Object.freeze({
    start,
    stop
  });
}

const timer = Timer(getTodos, 2000);
```

```
timer.start();
```

Encapsulation

With **class** all members, fields and methods, of the object are public.

With closures only the **start()** and **stop()** methods are public.
The **timerId** and **executeAndStartTimer()** are private.

Immutable public interface

The public interface of an object created with **class** can be modified.

```
const timer = new Timer(getTodos,2000);
timer.start = function() {
  console.log("don't start");
}
timer.start(); //"don't start"
```

The public interface of an object created with closures and
Object.freeze() is immutable.

No this

this may unexpectedly lose context when the method is used as a callback.
It may lose context when used in nested functions.

Consider the next example where **this** loses context when
executeAndStartTimer() is used as a callback.

```
executeAndStartTimer(){
   this.callback().then(() => {
      this.timerId =
      setTimeout(this.executeAndStartTimer, this.interval);
   });
 }
```

When the **start()** method is used as an event handler, like in the code
below, **this** loses context:

```
$("#btnStart").click(timer.start);
```

There are no such issues when using closures as **this** is not used.

JavaScript without **this** looks like a better functional programming language.

Stack

Stack is a data structure with two principal operation: push() for adding an element to the collection, and pop() for removing the most recent element added. It adds and removes elements according to the LIFO, Last In First Out, principle.

Look at the next example:

```
const stack = Stack();
stack.push(1);
stack.push(2);
stack.push(3);
stack.pop(); //3
stack.pop(); //2
```

Let's implement the stack with closures:

```
function Stack(){
  const list = [];

  function push(value){
    list.push(value);
  }

  function pop(){
    return list.pop();
  }

  return Object.freeze({
    push,
    pop
  });
}
```

The stack object has two public methods push() and pop(). The internal state can only be changed through these methods.

We can't modify directly the internal state:

```
const stack = Stack();
stack.list = null;
//Cannot add property list, object is not extensible
```

Queue

Queue is a data structure with two principal operations: `enqueue()` for adding an element to the collection, and `dequeue()` for removing the first element from the collection. It adds and removes elements according to the FIFO, First In First Out, principle.

Here is an example:

```
const queue = Queue();
queue.enqueue(1);
queue.enqueue(2);
queue.enqueue(3);
queue.dequeue(); //1
queue.dequeue(); //2
```

Take a look at a queue implemented with closures:

```
function Queue(){
  const list = [];

  function enqueue(value){
    list.push(value);
  }

  function dequeue(){
    return list.shift();
  }

  return Object.freeze({
    enqueue,
    dequeue
  });
}
```

As we have seen before, the internal state of the object can't be accessed from the outside.

Event emitter

An event emitter is an object with a publish/subscribe public interface. It is used to communicate between different parts in an application.

Look at the next example:

```
const eventEmitter = EventEmitter();

eventEmitter.subscribe("update", doSomething);
eventEmitter.subscribe("update", doSomethingElse);
eventEmitter.subscribe("add", addItem);

eventEmitter.publish("update", {});

function doSomething(value) { }
function doSomethingElse(value) { }
function addItem(value) { }
```

First, we subscribe with two functions for the **update** event, and with one function for the **add** event. When the event emitter publishes the **update** event, doSomething() and doSomethingElse() will be called.

Here is an implementation of a simple event emitter:

```
import partial from "lodash/partial";

function EventEmitter(){
  const subscribers = [];

  function subscribe(type, callback){
    subscribers[type] = subscribers[type] || [];
    subscribers[type].push(callback);
  }

  function notify(value, fn){
    try {
      fn(value);
    }
    catch(e) { console.error(e); }
  }

  function publish(type, value){
    if(subscribers[type]){
      subscribers[type].forEach(partial(notify, value));
    }
  }

  return Object.freeze({
```

```
    subscribe,
    publish
  });
}
```

Only the `publish()` and `subscribe()` methods are public. Everything else is private. `this` is not used.

Memory

Classes are better at memory conservation, as they are implemented over the prototype system. All methods will be created once in the prototype object and shared by all instances.

The memory cost of using closures is noticeable when creating thousands of the same object. Here is a measurement of the memory cost in Chrome:

Instances	10 methods	20 methods
10	0	0
100	~0.1 Mb	~0.1 Mb
1000	~0.7 Mb	~1.4 Mb
10000	~7 Mb	~14 Mb

Composition over inheritance

Factory functions promote composition over inheritance. Take a look at the next example where `SpecialService` reuses members of `Service` :

```
function Service() {
  function doSomething(){
    console.log("do-something");
  }

  return Object.freeze({
    doSomething
  });
}

function SpecialService({ service }){
  function doSomethingElse(){
    console.log("do-something-else");
```

```
  }

  return Object.freeze({
    doSomething : service.doSomething,
    doSomethingElse
  });
}

const specialService = SpecialService({
  service : Service()
});

specialService.doSomething();
//"do-something"

specialService.doSomethingElse();
//"do-something-else"
```

Final thoughts

Closures open a new way for doing object oriented programming without classes or prototypes.

Objects built with closures are encapsulated, favor composition and have not **this** changing context issues.

Chapter 15: Method decorators

> The decorators act like keywords or annotations, documenting the method's behavior but clearly separating these secondary concerns from the core logic of the method.— Reginald Braithwaite, author of JavaScript Allongé

Method decorators are a tool for reusing common logic. They are complementary to object oriented programming. Decorators encapsulate responsibility shared by different objects.

Consider the following code:

```
function TodoStore(currentUser){
  const todos = [];

  function add(todo){
    const start = Date.now();
    if(currentUser.isAuthenticated()){
      todos.push(todo);
    } else {
      throw new Error("Not authorized");
    }

    const duration = Date.now() - start;
    console.log("add() duration : " + duration);
  }

  return Object.freeze({
    add
  });
```

```
}

const currentUser = {
  isAuthenticated : function(){
    return true;
  }
}

const todoStore = TodoStore(currentUser);
todoStore.add({ title : "learn"});
//"add() duration : 0"
```

The `add()` method has the primary responsibility of adding a new `todo` to the internal state and two secondary responsibilities of authorizing the user and logging the duration of execution. The secondary concerns can repeat in other methods.

Imagine we decompose the secondary responsibilities in two function decorators with intention revealing names : `authorize()` and `logDuration()`. Then we compose everything together to create the original function.

```
import { compose } from "./tools";
import { logDuration, authorize } from "./decorators";

function TodoStore(){
  const todos = [];

  function add(todo){
    todos.push(todo);
  }

  return Object.freeze({
    add: compose(logDuration, authorize)(add)
  });
}
```

Now the `add()` method just adds the `todo` to the list. The other responsibilities are implemented by decorating the method.

Logging duration

A common scenario is logging the duration of a method call. The following decorator logs the duration of a synchronous call.

```
function logDuration(fn){
  return function(...args){
    const start = Date.now();
    const result = fn(...args);
    const duration = Date.now() - start;
    console.log(fn.name + "() duration : " + duration);
    return result;
  }
}
```

Authorization

The authorize() decorator makes sure the user has the rights to execute the method. This decorator is more complex as it has a dependency on another object currentUser. In this case, we can use a function createAuthorizeDecorator() to build the decorator. The decorator will execute the original method only if the user is authenticated.

```
function createAuthorizeDecorator(currentUser) {
  return function authorize(fn) {
    return function(...args) {
      if (currentUser.isAuthenticated()) {
        return fn(...args);
      } else {
        throw new Error("Not authorized");
      }
    };
  };
}
```

Now, we can create the decorator and pass the dependency.

```
const authorize = createAuthorizeDecorator(currentUser);
```

Decorator composition

Often we need to apply multiple decorators on a method. A simple way is to call the decorators one after the other:

```
function add() { }

const addWithAuthorize= authorize(add);
const addWithAuthorizeAndLog= logDuration(addWithAuthorize);
```

```
addWithAuthorizeAndLog();
```

Another way is to compose all decorators and then apply the new decorator on the original function.

```
import { compose } from "./tools";

const composedDecorator = compose(logDuration, authorize);
const addWithComposedDecorator = composedDecorator(add);
addWithComposedDecorator();
```

Below the `compose()` function is used to apply decorators on the `add()` method:

```
import { compose } from "./tools";

function TodoStore(){
  function add(){}

  return Object.freeze({
     add: compose(logDuration, authorize)(add)
  });
}

const todoStore = TodoStore();
todoStore.add();
```

Decorator order

In some cases, the order in which decorators get executed may not be important. But often the order does matter.

In our example, they are executed from left to right:

- 1st, the duration log starts
- 2nd, the authorization is performed
- 3rd, the original method is called

Decorating all object's methods

In some cases, we may need to apply decorators on all public methods of an object. We can create the `decorateMethods()` function to apply decorators on all public methods of an object.

```
function decorateMethods(obj, ...decorators) {
  const newObject = { ...obj };
  Object.keys(newObject).forEach(function(fnName) {
    if (typeof newObject[fnName] === "function") {
      newObject[fnName] =
          compose(...decorators)(newObject[fnName]);
    }
  });
  return newObject;
}
```

We may want to apply the decorators directly on the function that creates
the object. The `decorate()` function can help with that:

```
function decorate(factory, ...decorators) {
  return function(...args) {
    const newObject = decorateMethods(factory(...args),
                                      ...decorators);
    return Object.freeze(newObject);
  };
}
```

In the next example, all public methods of the object created by `TodoStore`
are decorated with `logDuration()` and `authorize()`.

```
import { decorate } from "./tools";
import { logDuration, authorize } from "./decorators";

function TodoStore(){
  function get(){}
  function add(todo){ }
  function edit(id, todo){}
  function remove(id){}

  return Object.freeze({
      get,
      add,
      edit,
      remove
  });
```

```
export default decorate(TodoStore, logDuration, authorize);
```

Store with pure functions

With decorators we can separate pure from impure code. Consider the following example:

```
export default function TodoStore() {
  let todos = [];

  function add(todos, todo) {
    return todos.concat([todo]);
  }

  function addAndMutate(todo) {
    todos = add(todos, todo);
  }

  return Object.freeze({
    add: addAndMutate
  });
}
```

In this case add() is a pure function and addAndMutate() is impure. In order to modify the todos state, we need to use the impure function. What if we encapsulate the impure code in a decorator like the setter below:

```
import { decorateMethods } from "./tools";

function Store(storeConfig) {
  return function() {
    let state = storeConfig.state;

    function setter(fn) {
      return function(...args) {
        state = fn(state, ...args);
      };
    }

    function getter(fn) {
      return function(...args) {
```

```
      return fn(state, ...args);
    };
  }

  return Object.freeze({
    ...decorateMethods(storeConfig.getters, getter),
    ...decorateMethods(storeConfig.setters, setter)
  });
  };
}

export default Store;
```

getter() takes a pure function and creates a function that returns the current state transformed with the pure function.

setter() takes a pure function and creates a function that modifies the state using the pure function.

With a library like Store.js we can write the TodoStore using only pure functions:

```
import Store from "./Store";

function add(todos, todo) {
  return todos.concat([todo]);
}

export default Store({
  state: [],
  setters: { add }
});
```

When running todoStore.add({ title: "verify" }), the setter() decorator calls the add() pure function with the current state as the first parameter and the new todo as the second parameter. Then, the setter() decorator uses the result to change the state.

Final thoughts

Decorators encapsulate common logic reusable between objects. They are complementary to object oriented programming.

Decorators improve readability. The code is much cleaner as it focuses on the main responsibility without being blurred by the secondary logic.

Chapter 16: Waiting for the new programming paradigm

Knowledge builds on knowledge.— John Carmack

JavaScript makes functional programming popular and offers a new way of building encapsulated objects with closures. While waiting for the new programming paradigm let's see what got us here.

OOP with classes

In 1985 C++ came out and added classes to the C language. Classes define the data and behavior of objects. Objects are instances of classes. Class members can be **private**, **protected** or **public**.

In 1995 Java, one of the most successful programming languages, was lunched. Classes are the basic unit of code, everything should be inside a class. In a class, **this** references the current object.

Let's create a **TodoStore** class that manages a list of **todos**. The **TodoStore** class has a private list and two public methods: **push()** and **getBy()**. The **Todo** class defines the **todo** transfer object. The two classes are then use in the **main()** function.

```
import java.util.List;
import java.util.ArrayList;
import java.util.stream.Collectors;

public class TodoStore
{
    private List<Todo> list;
```

```java
  public TodoStore()
  {
    this.list = new ArrayList<Todo>();
  }

  public void push(Todo todo)
  {
    list.add(todo);
  }

  public List<Todo> getBy(String text)
  {
    return list.stream()
      .filter(todo -> todo.Title.contains(text))
      .collect(Collectors.toList());
  }
}

public class Todo
{
  public Integer Id;
  public String Title;

  public Todo(Integer id, String title)
  {
    this.Id = id;
    this.Title = title;
  }
}

public class StartApplication
{
  public static void main(String[] args)
  {
    TodoStore todoStore = new TodoStore();

    todoStore.push(new Todo(1, "find"));
    todoStore.push(new Todo(2, "read"));
    todoStore.push(new Todo(3, "share"));
```

```
      List<Todo> filterTodos = todoStore.getBy("read");
      System.out.print("Count:" + filterTodos.size());
   }
}
```

Classes brought encapsulation.

Encapsulation means information hiding. It is about hiding as much as possible of the object's internal parts and expose a minimal public interface.

OOP with prototypes

In 1987 the Self language was released. It aimed to simplify class inheritance by replacing classes with prototypes. Objects can inherit from other objects. Self was a dynamically typed, prototype-based experimental language.

In 1995 the JavaScript language was created. In a way it put together the prototypes patterns ideas from the Self language with the functional patterns from Scheme, in a Java-like syntax.

class in JavaScript is sugar-syntax for creating objects with a custom prototype. Let's remake the previous TodoStore using prototypes:

```
class TodoStore{
  constructor(){
    this.list = [];
  }

  push(todo){
    this.list.push(todo);
  }

  getBy(text){
    return this.list
              .filter(todo => todo.title.includes(text));
  }
}

class Todo{
  constructor(id, title){
    this.id = id;
```

```
    this.title = title;
  }
}

(function startApplication(){
  const todoStore = new TodoStore();

  todoStore.push(new Todo(1, "find"));
  todoStore.push(new Todo(2, "read"));
  todoStore.push(new Todo(3, "share"));

  const filterTodos = todoStore.getBy("read");
  console.log("Count:" + filterTodos.length);
})();
```

The prototype system is more flexible than classes and is good at memory conservation, but it turns out to have some drawbacks:

- No encapsulation. All members, data and methods, are public.
- The public interface of the object is mutable. It can be changed from the outside.
- The need to manage the **this** losing context problems.

Functional programming

JavaScript rediscovered and brought to mainstream the functional programming paradigm.

Functional programming is better at solving some of our problems. It becomes clear that it is better at making code easier to read and understand and it is better at dealing with data transformations.

Programming in a functional style means to use concepts of functional programming such as first-class functions, closures, higher-order functions, partial application, immutability or pure functions.

Pure functional programming is a programming paradigm that treats all functions as pure functions.

Pure functions have a big set of advantages. They are easier to read understand, test, debug or compose. Pure functions are great, but we can't write a practical application using only pure functions.

OOP with closures

JavaScript brings closures to mainstream. Closures can encapsulate state. Even more, we can create multiple closures sharing the same private state. This way we can create flexible, encapsulated objects. Consider the next implementation of `TodoStore`:

```
function TodoStore(){
  const list = [];

  function push(todo){
    list.push(todo);
  }

  function getBy(text){
    return list.filter(todo => todo.title.includes(text));
  }

  return Object.freeze({
    push,
    getBy
  })
}

function Todo(id, title){
  return Object.freeze({id, title});
}

(function startApplication(){
    const todoStore = TodoStore();

    todoStore.push(Todo(1, "find"));
    todoStore.push(Todo(2, "read"));
    todoStore.push(Todo(3, "share"));

    const filterTodos = todoStore.getBy("read");
    console.log("Count:" + filterTodos.length);
})();
```

Objects built this way have a set of advantages :

- Encapsulation. Only the methods exposed are public, everything

else is hidden.
- Immutable public interface.
- No `this` related problems and complexity.
- Promote composition over inheritance.

Douglas Crockford pioneered the idea of splitting objects inside an application in two:

- Data objects that expose data and have no behavior. Data objects are immutable. They are created with the `Todo()` function in this example.
- Behavior objects that expose behavior and hide data. There is only one object in this example and is created with the `TodoStore()` function.

From a different perspective:

- Data objects are immutable collections of primitives or other plain objects
- Behavior objects are immutable collections of closures sharing the same private state

Final thoughts

Object oriented programming, functional programming, pure functional programming are all paradigms at our disposal for building better applications.

Functional programming turns out to be better at data transformations and making code easier to understand. Pure functions offer a solution to many of our problems and help creating code easier to read, understand, test, debug, compose. Nevertheless, functional programming doesn't seem to solve all challenges. Objects look to be better at encapsulating side effects and managing state.

The prototype system tries to simplify class inheritance but it turns out it has its own problems. It has no encapsulation and `this` creates losing context issues. However, the prototype system is good at memory conservation and is flexible enough to transpile class-based objects to prototype-based objects. In the end, the prototype system is good for transpiling reasons, making JavaScript a target compilation language.

JavaScript brings another way of creating objects as collections of closures This way is class-less, prototype-less. Using functions to build encapsulated objects fits better with the functional programming style.

While waiting for the new better programming paradigm we can use a mix of both functional and object oriented programming, trying to get the best of both worlds.

About the author

Cristian Salcescu is a Technical Lead passionate about front-end development and enthusiastic about sharing ideas. He took different roles and participated in all parts of software creation. Cristian Salcescu is a JavaScript trainer and a writer on Medium. He created training programs and knowledge sharing groups inside organizations.

47469699R00088

Made in the USA
Middletown, DE
07 June 2019